THE OBSERVER'S
POCKET SERIES

. . .

THE OBSERVER'S BOOK OF
HERALDRY ✐ ✐ ✐

The Observer's Books

THE OBSERVER'S BOOK OF

HERALDRY

By
Charles MacKinnon
of Dunakin
F.R.S.A., F.S.A. Scot.

*With 12 plates in full colour
and 118 line drawings*

FREDERICK WARNE & CO. LTD.
FREDERICK WARNE & CO. INC.
LONDON · NEW YORK

LIBRARY OF CONGRESS CATALOG
CARD NO. 67–10967

7232 0083 1

*Printed in Great Britain by
Cox & Wyman Ltd., London, Reading and Fakenham*
1033.368

CONTENTS

LIST OF PLATES

PREFACE

THIS is a brief survey of heraldry in Great Britain, its present state and how it got that way. I hope it will prove generally interesting to readers. In addition, those chapters which deal with the rules of heraldry may be a useful first step to the student who is new to this absorbing subject, and who wishes to know more about it.

Heraldry is part of our heritage in Great Britain. It is a matter of keen interest that in this ultra-modern age, when changes are many and sweeping, and when, as never before, people have reason to say that things are not as they were in the good (bad?) old days, the popularity of a subject as "reactionary" as heraldry is greater than it has ever been. No doubt sociologists can think of a clever reason for this; to me it suggests simply that the changes are not as deep as they often seem to be.

Without prying too deeply into the human mind, I think there is no doubt that heraldry appeals to some basic and deep-rooted appetite in mankind. We may be well aware that we are far better off as we are; but we still hanker after the pageantry of armour, swords, fluttering pennons, perfect and gentle knights (who were as rare then as they are now), and shields charged with their armorial bearings.

I hope, therefore, that at least some of the readers will derive as much genuine pleasure from this book as I did from the writing of it.

Struy, CHARLES MACKINNON OF DUNAKIN.
Inverness-shire.

PUBLISHER'S NOTE

The majority of the illustrations for this book have been taken from *Boutell's Heraldry* by C. W. Scott-Giles, O.B.E. and J. P. Brooke-Little, F.S.A., which is a more detailed and comprehensive work on the science of heraldry, and the reader who wishes to continue his studies in this field is recommended to consult this volume.

Thanks are given to the Heraldry Society for their kind permission to use the illustration on page 27. The illustration on page 34 was reproduced from *Guide to Heraldry* by A. C. Fox-Davies, published by Thomas Nelson and Sons Ltd.

WHAT IS HERALDRY?

IT is always a good thing to begin by getting defini-
tions right. In the case of heraldry this is more
difficult than we might suppose. It is not sufficient
to turn to the dictionary, where it is described as
"the art or office of the herald". This is unsatis-
factory because it begs the question and also because, in fact, the office of herald is considerably
older than what we now call heraldry. The dictionary goes on to say that it is the science of recording genealogies and blazoning coats of arms,
and this is getting a little closer to the mark; but
there are many ways of recording genealogies, of
which heraldry is only one, and blazoning is only
a part of the science of heraldry.

One text-book on heraldry has a sub-title describing heraldry as a medieval system of record
and identification and this, although it is not very
descriptive, is more accurate than the dictionary
definition. Heraldry *is* medieval in origin and *is*
concerned with identification. My own definition
of heraldry would be that it is a system of identifying individuals by means of hereditary devices
placed upon a shield, which system originated in
Western Europe in medieval times.

I am not suggesting this is a particularly clever
definition, although I think it is an adequate first

definition; but I would like to stress that one word, *hereditary*. As we shall see in the next chapter, marks have been borne on shields for a long time now, and for far longer than we have had heraldry. The thing that transforms them from idle decoration into the science of heraldry is the fact that they are handed on from father to son and so identify the *individual* in relation to his family. Properly applied, heraldry is a very exact and precise system of identification, infinitely more satisfactory than any system of names; and a heraldic seal is of much greater value than a mere signature since it gives a wealth of detail about the individual.

Heraldry then is a precise method of identification and is concerned with shields. Indeed, although a heraldic achievement consists of several components of which the shield is only one, there can be nothing without the shield. The shield, however, may be the only item in the achievement. The shield with its devices is therefore the very hub and kernel of the whole business, and the identification lies in the shield from which alone the individual may be recognized without reference to helmet, mantling, crest, motto or other adjuncts. This of course is one of the attractions of heraldry, that it is concerned primarily with gaily decorated shields which are bright and interesting. This attraction is particularly strong today when almost everybody is "entitled" to display some form of shield as a blazer badge.

There are some things which should be made clear about heraldry from the beginning.

1. *Seal of Thomas de Beauchamp, 3rd Earl of Warwick, 1344.*

It is not, as so many people wrongly imagine, an abstruse science. At one time it appeared so because its students smothered it in a wealth of meaningless and unnecessary detail, a good deal of which was in any case quite wrong.

Another fact which has tended to give people a wrong idea of heraldry is that it employs a vocabulary of its own. It is really a very brief and simple one which can be learned by heart in one day and never forgotten. Because, however, it is mostly in Norman French, because it is "technical", because it can be used by the intellectual snob to impress others who are not familiar with the terms of heraldry, it has added to the idea that this is the "closed-shop" of the super-expert. There are in fact considerably more technical terms involved in an ordinary motor-car engine than there are in the whole science of heraldry!

3

Yet another wrong idea about heraldry is that it is concerned only with the aristocracy. This is, to say the very least, a wild exaggeration. Coats of arms are, as it happens, a sign of technical nobility; but that does not mean that they are the exclusive property of the peerage, baronetage and knightage.

In the beginning arms were assumed purely to distinguish the persons and properties of individuals. The serf or peasant with no property had no cause to assume arms, and indeed in early times would not have been allowed to display them. From that point of view, therefore, there was a minimum standard below which arms were not used. It was a pretty modest standard financially, and has always remained so. The only money needed today is the money to pay for the grant of arms which, assuming that the petitioner is in no way "unworthy" by virtue of being demonstrably "ignoble", will probably be granted. There are far more coats of arms outside of the titled aristocracy of Britain than there are within it.

There is another side to heraldry altogether. Apart from grants made to individuals, arms are also granted to public bodies, corporations, cities, boroughs, schools, colleges, universities and so on (Plate 6). In Britain we are surrounded by heraldry from the day we are born till the day we die. It is to be found in castles, in cathedrals, on ashtrays, on public transport vehicles, on television screens, on signs outside inns, in the insignia of the Armed Forces of the Crown, in school, college and uni-

4

2. *University of Cambridge*

versity badges, on Government circulars, and outside the shops of tradesmen who have been granted the Royal Warrant and who proudly display heraldic achievements above the words "By appointment. . . ." One does not have to look far for heraldry in Britain. It is to be seen in almost every edition of all newspapers and magazines.

Heraldry, therefore, is not only *not* confined to the aristocracy, but because of its public as well as its private use, is of intense interest to everybody. It is bright and decorative as well as informative. It is not a "dead" subject—it is of practical use to architects, lawyers, artists and historians.

Oddly enough, although heraldry in its origin is bound up with monarchy and titles, the science has not declined in countries which have become republics. Both English and Scottish heralds can testify to the intense interest shown in America, and in countries such as France, where the monarchy has been overthrown, heraldry remains a living science. One of the most heraldic countries in the world is Switzerland, which is a republic.

It is indeed true to say that the interest in heraldry is more widespread today in the world in general than it has ever been during the entire history of the human race, and that this science, which many people still mistakenly believe to be the prerogative of a privileged aristocracy, flourishes in countries which have neither monarchy nor aristocracy. Dominions, Commonwealth countries and Crown Colonies all share in this interest, and oddly enough this includes countries which have recently attained independence. In Nigeria, for example, the people are tremendously proud of the country's coat of arms—granted by the English College of Heralds shortly before Nigeria became independent.

So we see heraldry not only as something colourful and appealing, but as something living, thriving and even expanding. It has in its time been the subject of snobbery and deliberately contrived misunderstanding. There have been efforts to turn it into an exclusive plaything for pseudo-aristocrats. Such efforts have failed. Heraldry has survived the transition into the atomic and space age. The Atomic Energy Authority has its properly matriculated arms, and no doubt the first Space Squadron of the Royal Air Force will have its squadron badge just as those other squadrons which once saw service in France with machines like Sopwith Camels and Maurice Farman Longhorns.

Heraldry, it seems, is here to stay, a fact which

would doubtless surprise the medieval knight in armour.

The purpose of this little book is to discover what it is all about and to examine briefly the few simple rules that govern it.

3. *Sir Winston Churchill*

CHAPTER I

THE BEGINNING OF HERALDRY

IN the introduction it was said that heraldry is a method of identification by means of hereditary marks borne on a shield. This fact has caused much misunderstanding because, of course, people have now been decorating shields for countless centuries; indeed since long before Christ. For that reason heraldry is often said to be much older than

R—O.B.H.—B 7

4. *Sir Roger de Setvans, c. 1305*

it actually is. Arms have been attributed to such unlikely people as Adam and Eve, Noah, Julius Caesar, the Pharaohs, Pontius Pilate and—more reasonably but equally wrongly—to the Normans at the time of their invasion of England in 1066. Even the Children of Israel have been charged with "having heraldry".

The truth is that heraldry is much more modern than all this, that it dates from the second quarter of the twelfth century, and that it is bound up with the development of armour in early medieval times. It is impossible to set down a definite date and say "heraldry began on such-and-such a date." Men have decorated their shields, as stated, for a long time. It is only when we find the same marks being repeated in the second generation, and being used as distinguishing marks of the individual *and his heirs*, that we can pinpoint the beginnings of heraldry. This evolution took place in Western Europe in the second quarter of the twelfth century, when armorial devices on shields began to be repeated and to be used for identification on seals, and so on. Within a remarkably short time the science had clearly taken shape and was conforming to its own rules.

It has long been the theory that the origins of heraldry lay in the use of the closed helmet, which rendered identification in battle virtually impossible. This, together with a general illiteracy, and combined with the growth of charters and paper-work generally, made a simple pictorial system of identification a practical necessity. Thus the knight or

9

other leader in battle decorated his shield and his surcoat—the cloth garment he wore over his armour to protect it from the hot sun and the rain—with symbols which identified him. The same man, when it became necessary to sign a document, affixed a seal to it which showed a figure on horseback. This figure had a surcoat and shield charged with his armorial bearings. Thus the illiterate knight "signed" the deed and thus his equally illiterate counterpart somewhere else was able to examine the seal and recognize the armorial bearings and know who it was who had signed the document. When we talk of King John signing the Magna Carta this is what we mean; he and the barons *sealed* it with armorial seals.

The origins of heraldry were then intensely practical. There was no "social" value in armorial bearings. Of course when the father died his son inherited the arms, otherwise the system could never have worked. It would have been impossible to keep track of the arms if everybody altered them at will. Once the thing got going, its use was immediately apparent. Alliances and feudal ties could be indicated by heraldic symbols. Not only the fighting men, but all persons who had business necessitating the "signing" of documents—churchmen, important and unimportant landowners, and so on—found that hereditary arms provided the solution to their problem. The growth of the science was rapid and by 1300 it had reached a highly developed state, as the early heraldic Rolls indicate.

It is interesting to note that it was only when the

5. *Seal of Humphrey de Bohun, Earl of Hereford, 1320*

symbols used in the mid-twelfth century began to be repeated later that century that heraldry received its birth impetus, and that there was *no such thing* as heraldry at the time of the Norman Conquest, or at the time of the First and Second Crusades. Before the adoption of hereditary symbols in the mid-twelfth century, the symbols which were used were displayed more or less at will by the individual, and were changed during his lifetime. They had no special significance except possibly over a short period, and conformed to no particular rules.

In the beginning it was essentially a utilitarian science, a matter of identifying knights and other war-leaders in battle. It had a certain social significance, of course, even then. The ordinary man-at-arms needed no particular identification and his concern was to follow his leader closely. If every foot-soldier had carried a banner the result would have been chaotic if colourful. The social significance, however, was incidental. There was certainly no "snob" value in the beginning and even the spread to peaceful purposes was dictated by necessity rather than the desire to cut a figure in society. It was only much later on that people began to differentiate between those who could claim a right to arms and those who could not. They became a symbol of ancient lineage. But by this time armory—which is the old word for what we now call heraldry—was in its first decline.

At the present time the word heraldry is one of romance, conjuring up as it does pictures of knights in armour, fair maidens, turreted castles, tournaments and deeds of honour. In this lies part of the secret of the appeal of heraldry today, because it is a living link with the past and with a particularly romantic part of the past.

This, then, is the popular and generally accepted account of the origins of heraldry: i.e., the threefold influence of (*a*) full armour and the closed helmet (*b*) illiteracy and (*c*) the increase in administrative work involving charters requiring signature. It is possible, however, that it was in the tournament rather than on the battlefield that the need for identification was greater, and that heraldry owes its inception more to mock-warfare and also the need to demonstrate royal and international marriage links.

In order to explain this it is necessary to understand the different use of titles. In the Western feudal system a title belonged to one man only, and this is still the case. Thus, although in Scotland there are many Campbells, and many of them are peers, there is only one Duke of Argyll. The arms of all other Campbells, no matter how closely related or how high they stand in the peerage, must be different from those of the Duke, and also different from each other.

In East Frankish lands, however, a title belonged to a family. For example, all the kinsmen of the Duke of Arenberg are themselves Dukes of Arenberg, and they will all use the same coat of arms.

In other words, in the west a man would be an earl, not his kindred. In Germanic countries, however, the whole family would be earls, all equally sharing the earldom, the title and the arms. Thus Ernst, *Herzog* zu Braunschweig und Luneberg is the brother of Georg, *Herzog* zu Braunschweig und Luneberg, and uncle of Welf, *Herzog* zu Braunschweig und Luneburg. In fact there are at present no less than seven living Dukes of Brunswick and Luneburg. Similarly all members of the house of Wettin are styled Duke of Saxony— Herzog von Sachsen.

Thus at the very dawn of heraldry, and in the most influential part of Christian Europe—the Holy Roman Empire—a dozen or more members of the same family would all wear the same arms. In local wars and family quarrels there might easily be three Wettins in battle against four other Wettins, all squabbling kinsmen, all wearing exactly the same coat of arms.

Obviously, therefore, although full armour might have rendered heraldry particularly useful in West Frankish lands, it did not make much difference in the East. It cannot be entirely true to say, as is often said, that heraldry owes its birth to the difficulty of recognizing in battle a man wearing a helmet and visor.

Therefore it is possible that the theory of the tournament is correct. There each knight hung his shield before his pavilion, was announced by his name and titles, and performed before spectators who wanted to know where their favourite was once the visors were closed. The inconvenience of a number of knights all in tournament armour, complete with pot helms, all taking part in simultaneous exercises, and lacking any identification is easy to imagine—rather like a football international with both sides wearing identical jerseys and shorts, and no numerals.

The subject has not yet been fully covered, and still occupies the time and attention of experts. Whatever the reason, the fact remains that the world was ready for *some* system of identification, and heraldry provided the answer.

People sometimes ask if heraldry ever existed outside Western Europe. There seems to be no real trace of it anywhere, at any rate in a developed form. In Japan there is a system of hereditary crests called "Mons", used by Japanese peers. It is a rudimentary system compared with heraldry. There have been cases in Greek and Roman times of men using the same symbols and signs on their shields as their father used. This may have been out of respect, or else "for luck" particularly if the father was a renowned warrior of whom one would be particularly proud. But there was never a *system* of identifying the individual and indicating his ancestry.

There may have been primitive systems similar to the Japanese Mon system, but if so they have not lived on and they could never have reached any advanced state or else some trace would have survived.

Whatever may have occurred in the ancient past, we are left with the fact that heraldry as we know it originated in Western Europe in medieval times; and whatever might have been the main factor in its inception it was immediately adopted for use in tournament, in battle, for "signature" and for the pictorial recording of important dynastic alliances and royal marriage ties. All these things played their important part in its origins. None of them is a reason for its present continuance, and it is strange to reflect that heraldry has grown and spread from Western Europe to the New World, and that it is a living science in this century. It is now put to much more widespread practical use than ever before in its history, and from a decorative point of view it has in the twentieth century invaded millions of homes through the media of blazer badges and wall plaques.

CHAPTER II

THE COAT OF ARMS

THE "coat" of arms was actually the linen surcoat worn over the armour to protect it from the direct rays of the sun. In the heraldic period this garment came to be decorated on the front and back with the arms exactly as they were on the shield. This was the original and proper coat of arms and of course it has no existence today except in the beautifully embroidered tabards of the heralds.

Most people use the expression coat of arms quite indiscriminately to indicate either a shield (in which case they are using it more or less accurately), or the crest, or else the whole heraldic achievement, which is the shield with all its adjuncts, and in the last two cases the term coat of arms is wrong. The correct expression for the whole thing is the "achievement".

An achievement normally consists of the following six basic parts. They are called basic because they are in fact the basis of *most* modern achievements; but it is worth noting here that they are not all necessary. The only thing without which nothing else can exist is the shield, and this in a few rare cases is the only item in the achievement—if this is so you may be sure that it is very ancient indeed.

6. *MacKinnon of Dunakin*

For some considerable time now, the following items have been granted:

(a) the shield, often simply called "the arms" and sometimes the "coat of arms"
(b) the helmet
(c) the mantling or lambrequin
(d) the wreath or torse
(e) the crest
(f) the motto

To these basic parts there might be added, by reason of rank and honour, any or all of the following extra parts or additions:

(a) a cap of maintenance, or *chapeau*

17

(b) a crest coronet

(c) supporters

(d) a compartment

(e) a slogan

(f) a standard or ensign

(g) a coronet of rank (in the case of peers)

(h) the insignia of orders of chivalry

(i) a badge

From this it can be seen that a complete achievement may be a very complex and ornamental thing indeed (see Fig. 12, page 27).

The Shield This, as stated, is the literal basis of the whole thing, and without it there can be no other part of the achievement. It may be of almost any shape imaginable, from a plain circle to the most elaborately scalloped outline. A good deal depends on the fancy of the artist. Sometimes the shield is displayed with a "bouche" or piece cut out of the dexter side to allow for the free movement of the lance in the tournament.

Fashions and styles influence heraldry just as they do the other pictorial arts, and there have been clearly defined periods in heraldic art, not all of which were good.

The shield may be shown in an upright position, or hanging slantwise below the helmet. The latter is the more correct position for this is how the shield would have hung naturally from a peg in medieval times, and official heraldic artists use this slantwise ("couche") position quite a lot.

The size of the shield varies and at its worst it

7. *Bouché-shaped shield* 8. *Heater-shaped shield at Witworth*

appears as about six or eight times the size of the helmet. This is nonsense, of course, as no shield was ever this size in heraldic times—though at a much earlier period the shield did cover the whole body. The correct proportion of shield to helmet is almost half and half, the helmet being only just smaller than the shield.

The neatest shape of shield and one most widely used nowadays is called the "heater" type which is about one third longer than it is broad and which has plain outlines coming to a neat point at the base.

The surface of the shield is called the "field", and certain figures called "charges" are arranged on this field. A few very ancient families have shields consisting only of a field which has been divided into two or more colours or metals, and which bear no charges. This is extremely rare and in the vast majority of cases there is a charge, or charges, on the shield. In describing the shield and its charges we are "blazoning" it. Painting it from the "blazon" or description is called "emblazoning" (Plate 3).

The Helmet There is perhaps no part of the heraldic achievement which has led to so much bad artistry as the helmet. The real helmet was almost as large as the shield, and in an achievement it is shown placed on top of the shield, except in the case of peers who show it placed on top of their coronet. In a great many Victorian drawings the helmets are so peculiar that the human head could never have got into them. The various types of helmet as used in heraldry are:

(a) Royal helmet, which is always shown facing the front. The opening is guarded by grilles or bars. It is all gold.

(b) Peers' helmets, which also have bars or grilles, but the helmet is silver and the bars gold, and the helmet is shown in profile and not *affronté*.

(c) Baronets' and Knights' helmets, which are of steel with an open visor, and face the front. The garnishings are usually of gold.

(d) Esquires' and gentlemen's helmets, which are steel and have closed visors, and are shown in profile.

The fact that the helmets already mentioned have visors or grilles means that the tilting helm cannot be used for them, but the classifications given above are no longer rigidly adhered to nowadays. When the helmet is in profile it is always turned to the dexter side.

At this point we must stop and explain about dexter and sinister. Dexter means right, and sinister means left. In heraldry, however, they refer to the right and left of *the wearer* of the shield, not the onlooker. Therefore when we talk about a helmet facing the dexter, it is actually facing the *left* and not the right, from our point of view as onlookers. As we seldom, if ever, have occasion to imagine ourselves standing behind an achievement, it is easier if we simply think of *dexter* as being *left* for all practical purposes, even if it literally means something different.

The principal type of helmet depicted nowadays,

9. *Great Helms*

outside the peerage where the helmet with grille is almost invariably shown, is the great helm or the tilting helm. Both these helms rest on the shoulders and are one-piece helmets which are placed squarely over the head. The main difference between them is that it was possible to look forwards out of the great helm. The tilting helm, however, was so designed that it was only possible to see out of it when bending forwards slightly, as in the crouching or attacking position adopted in tilting. This jousting or frog-mouthed helm provided excellent protection in the joust. The head was raised just before the instant of impact and so there was little chance of an enemy's lance piercing the eyepiece or *occularium*. The shape of the helm was such that the lance would be deflected away from it.

This helm is properly used by people of tournament rank, and knights and baronets often display

10. *Tilting helms from Cobham Church, Kent*

it nowadays instead of the open-visored helmet. A most interesting display of helmets by a modern heraldic artist is to be found in the *Map of Scotland of Old* compiled by Sir Iain Moncreiffe of that Ilk, Bt, Albany Herald, and illustrated by Don Pottinger, Unicorn Pursuivant.

Mantling or lambrequin The mantling was a cloth cape worn from the back of the helmet to protect the metal from the hot rays of the sun, and undoubtedly had its origin in the crusades even though there was no science of heraldry at the time of the first two crusades. In due course it came to be of the same colour as the principal colour of the shield, and its underside was the same as the principal metal—yellow and white representing gold and silver as metals.

Mantling nowadays usually displays the livery colours of the owner, which are the principal colour and metal. The mantling of peers, and of certain officers of state, is crimson lined with (or "doubled") ermine, even though the livery colours may be quite different. The mantling of the Royal family is gold doubled ermine. There are a few exceptions to the general rule. Sir Iain Moncreiffe, for instance, has mantling which is plain green and which is "slashed" so as to form his plant badge, the oak leaf. It is unique in Scotland.

In battle mantling naturally became torn after a time, and hung in ribbons. This naturally gave rise to the "old soldier" idea, and no doubt knights took pride in arriving home in suitably tattered and dilapidated mantling, showing that they had been on a crusade or a long campaign. It soon became the done thing to have mantling depicted in a slashed form in the achievement, and in the eighteenth and nineteenth centuries, when heraldic art was in a very poor state, the shield often looked like a plate floating on a bed of seaweed, so intricate was the fancy slashing of the mantling which surrounded it. Nowadays heraldic art has found a new and noble simplicity, and the tendency is to show the mantling unslashed or else to show a simple slashing which approximates more closely to the real thing. There is no rule as to how mantling must be shown, provided that it contrives to display the underside. It issues from the top of the helmet at the point where the wreath sits.

The Wreath The wreath is all too often shown as a sort of barber's pole, but it was in fact a circle of silk, with gold or silver cord twisted round it, and it was placed on the helmet to cover the joint between the crest and the mantling. It is always depicted in the achievement as being six twists of alternating metal and colour and was the means of fastening the crest to the helmet. Sometimes it is claimed that it is wrong to show the crest on its wreath, but this is not so, and the two things do go together.

The Crest If the helmet has given rise to bad artistry, the crest has given rise to the most amazing and widely held popular misunderstanding in the

24

11. *Daubygné, 1345.*
(Note proportion of shield and unfussy mantling)

whole science of heraldry. Countless people believe that they have a crest *even though they know very well that they have no coat of arms*. It is difficult to understand how this extraordinary state of affairs arose, but much of the blame must be attached to the nineteenth century heraldic stationers who encouraged the cult of the crest and who urged members of the public to write and enclose payment whereupon by return of post they would be given an authentic copy of their crest. This bogus traffic thrived for many years. The plain fact, however, is that the crest is a *part* of the heraldic achievement and cannot exist without the rest. It may, of course, be *displayed* on its own without any shield, but there must *be* a shield. No person who does not have a personal coat of arms can have a crest, any more than they can have liveries or supporters. It is still a very widespread custom for people to have crests engraved on signet rings when they ought not to do so.

Generally speaking, no grant of arms is now made without a crest, and only very old families can boast arms minus this component. The word crest is one of the much misused words of heraldry, people saying "crest" when they mean coat of arms, or achievement. The crest was actually worn on top of the helmet, and in the achievement it is shown in that position. On stationery or visiting cards it is frequently shown on its wreath, with the motto on a scroll below, and nothing else.

The Motto Anyone of course can adopt a motto. The motto under discussion is the official motto granted with arms, and which is shown in England on a scroll below the crest, and in Scotland on a scroll above the crest. Mottoes are very much a matter of personal taste. Some of the older ones are extremely interesting, some are obscure and meaningless, and others are stilted Latin tags. When the shield is shown by itself it is usual to place the motto on a scroll below it. There is no need to show the motto—the shield may be displayed alone.

These are the six basic items, and one thing is to be noticed. Several people quite unconnected by blood may have the same crest, or very similar crests; a great many have the same motto; thousands have the same combinations of metals and colours in their liveries. There is no absolute "copyright" in any of these things, although in the case of certain crests bearing peculiar marks

DEXTER   SINISTER

ENTALENTE·A·PARLER·DARMES

1. Shield	4. Torse	7. Mantling
2. Charge	5. Supporters	8. Motto
3. Helm	6. Crest	9. Badge

12. *The Heraldry Society*

assigned by heralds, or of certain mottoes referring to facts from family history or peculiar to the family, the heralds would refuse to allow any duplication. For instance no person in Scotland would be permitted to use the motto *Touch Not The Cat Bot A Glove* unless he was a member of the Clan Chatten confederation. It is the shield of arms, however, which is *always* different. Within the family the differences will be small ones, and may even be temporary ones, and the basis of the arms may be the same, thus demonstrating the link between one branch of a family and another. No two arms will be *exactly* the same, however, and this is a first principle of Britain's heraldry.

Next come the other parts of the achievement which may be granted in special cases.

The Chapeau The chapeau or cap of maintenance is sometimes granted instead of a wreath, and in that case the crest issues from it. It is a velvet cap lined with ermine and is used in England to denote peers. In Scotland it is the symbol of the feudal baronage, which still exists in Scotland and is nothing to do with peerage, and is therefore particularly useful for indicating the arms of barons who, not being peers of Parliament, are not entitled to coronets. There is considerable scope for indicating the type of barony by varying the colour of the cap, e.g., Gules doubled Ermine, Azure doubled Ermine, and so on.

The Crest Coronet This is sometimes called a ducal coronet, which is misleading as it has never been associated in Britain with any particular peerage rank. However, where an animal, particularly a supporter, is gorged with a coronet, it is then correctly described as "ducally gorged".

The crest coronet is a rare item in this country,

13. *Chapeau*

14. *Crest coronet*

although it is common enough in the rest of Europe. Possibly at one time it indicated personal attendance on the sovereign, and in Scotland it is now adjudged that the crest coronet of gold indicates the chief of a whole name and arms—i.e., "of that Ilk". Even so, by no means all chiefs have it, and it is never rematriculated for cadets, and is reserved for use only with the undifferenced arms. When it is granted it is displayed on top of the helmet, and the crest issues from it instead of from a wreath or chapeau. It consists of a circlet and four strawberry leaves, three of which are visible.

Supporters Supporters are a great honour in heraldry and are only granted in special cases. Everybody is familiar with the supporters of the Royal Arms—the lion and the unicorn. The original use of supporters is believed to have been very prosaic: when arms were shown on a round seal, there were blank spaces at each side and the artists filled in the spaces by depicting beasts supporting or holding up the shield.

Grants of supporters are nowadays limited to the following:

(a) Peers.

(b) Knights of the Garter, the Thistle or St Patrick.

(c) Knights Grand Cross and Knights Grand Commander of the other British sovereign orders.

(d) A few exceptional cases of persons of great renown who do not fall into the other classes.

Sometimes one finds quite obscure families, outside the peerage, using hereditary supporters. This is usually the result of some famous ancestor in the far past. Several families in England have this comparatively unusual distinction. When supporters are granted with a degree of knighthood as above, they are not hereditary but only apply to the person who holds the chivalric honour. For instance if a person is made a G.C.V.O. he will be given supporters, but although his son will succeed to his arms, he will *not* succeed to the supporters—unless, of course, he qualifies in his own right by becoming a Knight Grand Cross of an order, or receiving the Garter, or being created a peer.

In Scotland, in addition to the cases above, there is another class of person who has supporters—the hereditary chiefs, and in some cases chieftains, of the various "names". The definition of a chief in Scotland is, among other things, that he has hereditary supporters. Thus all chiefs of the whole name (*chefs du nom*) such as Cameron of Lochiel, MacGregor of MacGregor, Dundas of that Ilk and Moncreiffe of that Ilk all have supporters as heads of the whole of their name. Some of the greater chieftains also share this honour, but not many.

In Scotland supporters may be granted by the Lord Lyon King of Arms, not acting on a Royal Warrant as does the Earl Marshal in England, but entirely on his own authority. This unusual power granted to the Lord Lyon is not one of which he makes much use, for the award of supporters is a rare distinction and a high honour.

The Compartment It is a common practice nowadays to show the supporters standing on a suitable compartment, rather than to have them apparently hanging in mid-air from the sides of the shield. The details of the compartment are usually described in the grant of arms and sometimes there is a special feature involved—e.g., the Earl of Perth's compartment is strewn with a particularly unpleasant medieval gadget for laming horses, called a caltrap. This commemorates an event at the Battle of Bannockburn in 1314 when caltraps were strewn in the path of the English cavalry. Chiefs of Scottish clans usually have compartments strewn with their plant badge.

The Slogan In Scotland it is usual for the head of a great family, or the chief of a clan, to have a slogan as well as a motto, and it is then specified in the Public Register of All Arms and Bearings in Scotland. The slogan was the gathering cry of the chief when rallying his clan, and it is now confined to persons who have a considerable following.

Standards and Ensigns The use of standards and ensigns is very strictly controlled. The ensign is a small rectangular flag, fringed with bullion, and the ground shows the livery colours. On it is embroidered the whole achievement. The ensign was a personal flag.

The standard was used to display the owner's badge. It was a long narrow flag with split ends, and next to the staff (in the hoist) it displayed either the St George's or the St Andrew's cross. Since the Union it has become the custom to display the owner's arms in the hoist. After this follows the badge, crest and motto. The granting of standards and guidons, which are similar, is subject to a number of rules regarding the status of the person involved.

These heraldic flags are still in practical use in Scotland where at gatherings the chief's standard is set up before his tent, and is the rallying point for his clansmen, denoting as it does his headquarters. His ensign is usually displayed on the bagpipes carried by the chief's personal piper. His *banner*, which denotes his personal presence, is either hoisted on his arrival, or else he will be accompanied by a banner-bearer carrying it. The banner, which has sometimes been referred to as "a rectangular shield" is only awarded to peers, baronets and feudal barons

Coronets of Rank Peers display their coronets as part of their achievement. The coronet rests on top of the shield, below the helmet. There are coronets for each grade of the peerage, and a coronet comprises a cap of maintenance inside a circlet of gold, the pattern of which varies with rank (Plate 12).

> Royal duke: four strawberry leaves alternating with four fleurs-de-lis
>
> Duke: eight strawberry leaves
>
> Marquis: four balls on short spikes alternating with four strawberry leaves
>
> Earl: eight balls on tall spikes alternating with eight strawberry leaves
>
> Viscount: sixteen silver balls
>
> Baron (Lord of Parliament): six silver balls

Insignia of Orders of Chivalry When the owner of arms receives any order of chivalry he can display its insignia with his armorial bearings. Normally the circlet of the order goes round the shield and the badge is pendant from it. The circlet usually shows the motto of the order. In the case of Knights Grand Cross and Knights Grand Commander, the collar of the order is shown instead of a circlet—the same applies for orders like the Garter and Thistle, which can be seen on the Royal Arms in England and Scotland. Where several chivalric orders have been bestowed,

33

15. *Married Knight.*
(*Note the collar of his
Order of Knighthood
round his own shield,
together with another
shield showing his arms
impaled with his wife's*)

all can be displayed, the highest in importance
being nearest to the shield. Baronets of Nova
Scotia show the arms of Nova Scotia on a badge
suspended below the shield from an orange ribbon
(Plate 5). They also show the arms in a canton on
the shield itself.

This custom normally only applies to British
sovereign orders, and not to foreign orders unless
permission has been granted to wear and display
the insignia. However it also includes the Order of
the Hospital of St John of Jerusalem.

Badges Badges are sometimes granted to the
heads of great houses. Their purpose is to distinguish or "badge" the followers and retainers. The
badge is displayed on the standard, which is the

rallying flag of these followers. The badge never denotes the *person* of the leader, and it is only awarded to someone who has a large number of followers. Peers, barons, Scottish chiefs and some of the chieftains have badges, together with standards and slogans—the three usually going together.

Most people are familiar with national badges, such as the English rose, the Scottish thistle and also the St Andrew's cross badge, the Irish shamrock, and the Welsh daffodil and leek badges. When used in any official capacity, these national badges are ensigned with a crown (Plate 8).

These then are the components of the heraldic achievement. A visit to a public library and an hour or two with a Debrett or a Burke's Peerage will show all of them in use, and can do more to illustrate their beauty and purpose than any amount of description in a book.

In heraldry, as in other subjects, all sorts of "special cases" exist, which engage the attention of experts and provide a fascinating number of exceptions to rules. In a book of this nature no attempt will be made to deal with exceptions and special rules, and this book is therefore confined to general principles.

CHAPTER III

THE COLOURS AND DIVISIONS OF THE SHIELD

THE field of the shield, and the charges placed upon it, are all coloured, and the "colours" are classified into two *metals*, five *colours* and nine *furs*—all of which are termed "tinctures". The only exception to this is when some charges are displayed as "proper" meaning that they are coloured in their natural colours—e.g., an oak tree proper will have green foliage and a brown trunk and branches.

The two metals used in heraldry are gold and silver, and are usually represented by yellow and white although it would be more accurate to use metallic paints. The heraldic names for these metals (and for the other tinctures) are Norman French, for during the time heraldry was coming into existence, and for centuries afterwards, French was the language of the gentleman just as Latin was the language of the scholar and churchman. Not only are French words used, but also French construction, and the adjective *follows* the noun it describes. Furthermore in heraldry where more than one adjective is used, the tincture is given last.

The names for gold and silver are Or and Argent. If we have a gold boar's head it will be described

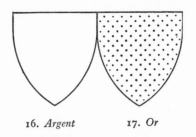

16. *Argent* 17. *Or*

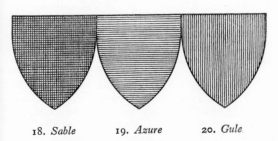

18. *Sable* 19. *Azure* 20. *Gule*

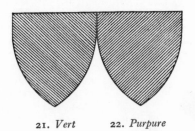

21. *Vert* 22. *Purpure*

37

as *A boar's head Or*. If it were *couped*, which is to say cut off cleanly at the neck instead of being jagged (*erased*) we would say *A boar's head couped Or*.

The colours used in heraldry are mostly primary colours and are:

Red, which is called Gules
Green, which is called Vert
Blue, which is called Azure
Purple, which is called Purpure
Black, which is called Sable

There are definite laid-down abbreviations for these tinctures, both metals and colours. There is a system of depicting them in black and white drawings by "hatching"; the direction of the lines indicates the various colours (page 37). Hatching is not really a very useful thing because where there is a great deal of detail on a shield it is almost impossible to shade it, and it is far better to show it in simple outline and attach a heraldic description. The table on page 39 shows the list of metals and colours.

There are two other colours but they are so rare that they are not worth trying to remember. They are Tenné and Sanguine, and are sometimes called "stains", Tenné being a tawny colour and Sanguine a peculiar shade of red.

There are more furs than colours, but here again there are only a few common ones and the rest are uncommon and not worth trying to memorize. The furs most frequently met with are Ermine, which is depicted by black spots on a white ground, Ermines which is white spots on a black ground, and

Heraldic Name:	Abbrev.	Hatching	Colour
Or	Or	dots	gold
Argent	Arg.	plain white	silver
Gules	Gu.	vertical lines	red
Azure	Az.	horizontal lines	blue
Vert	Vert	lines in bend (i.e., running from top left to bottom right)	green
Purpure	Purp.	lines in bend sinister (i.e., running from top right to bottom left)	purple
Sable	Sa.	vertical and horizontal lines crossing to form tiny squares	black

Vair which is meant to depict a squirrel skin and is conventionally shown by shield-shaped pieces in blue and white. This is said to be the fur of which Cinderella's slippers were made, and if the word had not been misread as "verre" the idea of a *glass* slipper would never have arisen.

The less common furs are Erminois which is black spots on a gold background, and Pean which is gold spots on black. These are both Ermine variants. There is also Counter-Vair, in which colour is placed against colour and metal against metal, and the bells point in different directions in the alternate rows. This is a type of Vair, as also is Vair in Pale, in which the bells are directly over one another instead of being staggered as in ordinary Vair. The final two furs are Potent and Counter-potent. Potent consists of alternate crutch-shaped pieces in blue and white, and counter-potent is a version of this in which alternate lines of crutches are reversed and placed point to point, giving a very peculiar result (see page 41).

There now enters on the scene the villain of the piece called the Rule of Tincture. Briefly stated, this says that a colour must never be placed on a colour, or a metal on a metal. Furs may be placed on either metal or colour, which makes them very useful indeed; they may not, however, be placed on other furs.

The purpose of this rule is to prevent confusion caused by shields which are not identifiable at a glance. For example, a black lion on a purple field would not be easy to pick out, and it would be even

23. *Ermine*   24. *Ermines*

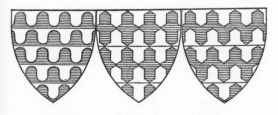

25. *Vair*   26. *Counter-Vair*   27. *Vair en point*

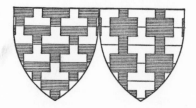

28. *Potent*   29. *Counter-Potent*

more difficult to decide whether it was rampant or salient, without getting very close. The object of heraldry was *easy* identification, hence the tincture rule.

The operative word in the rule is "on". Where a field simply is divided by a line of division, the parts are lying side by side, and the rule of tincture does not apply. Thus in the case of the arms in Fig. 6, page 17, the shield is *divided* per fess (i.e., across its centre) and the top half is green and the lower half is red. Both are colours and neither is "on" the other. But the *charges* on both halves are metal, for the rule of tincture applies to them. Note that had the boar's head been on a *chief*, the top of the shield could not have been green, for the chief is what is called an Ordinary, and it is placed *on* the shield.

There are certain exceptions to the Rule of Tincture which one must know. It does *not* apply when the field is a varied field—for example, a field might be barry wavy which means that it would be composed of undulating bars of alternate metal and colour. In this case the charges placed on the shield, whether metal or colour, in places will appear to break the rule. This cannot be helped. The technical breach of the rule is accepted and one can have a red dragon on a field which is a barry wavy of blue and white.

Another exception is made for the bordure, for the bordure may be divided into metals and colours, and here it again must conflict with parts of the field.

Yet another exception is made when certain

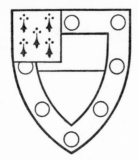

30. *Woodfield* – Per fess Gules and Argent, a bordure gold charged with 8 torteaux, over all a carton ermine

parts of animals are specially coloured—e.g., tongue, claws, beak, horns, mane, and so on. A silver boar's head on a green background can have a red tongue (in heraldry we would say it was "langued Gules") and this is the case in Fig. 6.

Finally the Rule of Tincture is occasionally broken deliberately. In very special cases, where the purpose is to confer unusual distinction on someone, this may be done. Such arms are rare. The standard-bearer of Henry V at Agincourt was reputedly granted a red fretty upon a black fess, as a reward. The idea was that this breach of the rule would make people inquire more closely into the arms and so serve to perpetuate the memory of the man's bravery. This is not a common thing in Britain. Agincourt was very much a special case with Henry V, who ever afterwards had a soft spot for those who fought with him there, and one can understand how in this case he would want to do something special.

The best known arms which break the rule of tincture are probably those of Jerusalem which consist of gold crosses on a silver field.

In addition to the different tinctures, there are different methods of dividing the field. The various points of the shield are illustrated in Fig. 31. Three of them are in chief and three in base, and the remaining three are (from top to bottom) the honour point, the fess point, and the nombril point. The divisions are:

Per pale	The shield is divided vertically up the middle.
Per fess	The shield is divided horizontally across the centre.
Per bend	The shield is divided diagonally from top left to bottom right, as we look at it.
	N.B. In all four of these divisions the lines pass through the fess point.
Per chevron	The shield is divided by a chevron, the apex of which reaches the honour point.
Quarterly	The shield is divided into four quarters, which is a double division per pale and per fess.
Per saltire	The shield is divided by a combination of two dividing lines, one in bend sinister, resulting in a "St Andrew's cross".
Gyronny	The field is divided into eight segments by lines in pale, fess,

44

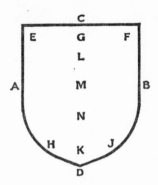

31. *Points of the shield:* a. *Dexter side* b. *Sinister side* c. *Chief* d. *Base* e. *Dexter chief* f. *Sinister chief* g. *Middle chief* h. *Dexter base* j. *Sinister base* k. *Middle base* l. *Honour point* m. *Fess point* n. *Nombril or Navel point*

bend and bend sinister. See Fig. 39, page 47.

These divisions all assume that straight lines are being used, and where this is so, no particular description of the lines themselves is given. *Per fess Azure and Argent* means that the shield is divided by a *straight* line running horizontally through the fess point and that the top is blue and the bottom silver or white. The lines, however, *need not be straight*, and Figs. 40–42, page 48 show some of the variations of dividing lines. There are several others, not illustrated, which are uncommon and do not concern us at this stage.

These variations all have their special heraldic names which must be used. Thus we might have *Per fess embattled, Argent and Azure*.

Before leaving this subject of the divisions of the field, we should consider how the arms are blazoned or described. Earlier mention was made of European arms which have a plain coloured field. A description such as "An escutcheon Argent" is beautifully simple, and presents no difficulty. Unfortunately there are far too many coats of arms for this, and in Britain only a small number have even a plain field with a single ordinary. The normal thing is to have a field with a division and one or more charges, at the very least. In some cases the arrangement or *marshalling* of the arms may be very complicated indeed.

To assist in making heraldry simple and internationally intelligible—which incidentally it is—rules of blazon have been evolved. They are not difficult and from a blazon a person who understands the subject can at once picture in his mind what the achievement looks like, and can draw and colour it. The main rules of blazon are:

1. *If the shield is quartered, this must be stated first of all*. After this the quarters will be described in turn, in order of sequence. If the fourth quarter is a repeat of the first this will be described as "Quarterly, 1st and 4th". For example, the Royal arms used in England are Quarterly, 1st and 4th England, 2nd Scotland, 3rd Ireland (Plate 1).

Where one or more quarters are themselves

46

32. *Per fess* 33. *Per pale* 34. *Per bend*

35. *Per bend sinister* 36. *Per chevron* 37. *Per cross,*
or quarterly

38. *Per saltire* 39. *Gyronny*

40.

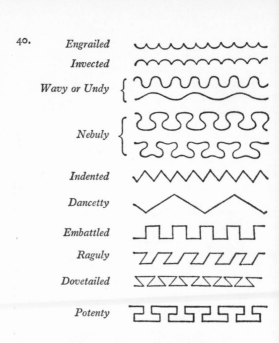

Engrailed	
Invected	
Wavy or Undy	
Nebuly	
Indented	
Dancetty	
Embattled	
Raguly	
Dovetailed	
Potenty	

41. *Engrailed figure* 42. *Invected figure*

quartered, the four main quarters are called grand-quarters, and each is dealt with in turn. Thus we might get something like:

"Quarterly. 1st grand quarter counter-quartered, 1st and 4th Azure a buckle Or, 2nd Gules a chevron Argent, 3rd Sable an antique crown Or; 2nd grand quarter Azure a bend Ermine; 3rd grand quarter counter-quartered, 1st Argent a stag's head cabossed Gules, 2nd Gules a pile Or, 3rd Ermine a lion rampant guardant Sable, 4th Or a bendlet Azure between three fountains; 4th grand quarter Sable a mullet Argent."

Note that the first word, no matter how simple or how complicated the blazon, is always "Quarterly".

2. *The field is described either by tincture or by division and tincture.* If we have a red shield charged with a silver five-pointed star, we would blazon it Gules, a mullet Argent. If the shield is divided we would say, "Per fess, Gules and Argent, in chief a mullet of the second." This means that the mullet is in the top half and is of the second tincture mentioned—i.e., Argent. If the mullet in this case were placed centrally on the fess point, part of it would fall in the half coloured Gules and part of it would be on the Argent half; and to conform to the rule of tincture the mullet would have to be counterchanged. This would make the top half of the mullet white and the bottom half red. For examples of counterchanging, see Figs. 44 and 45.

3. *The principal charge lying on the field is next*

49

43.

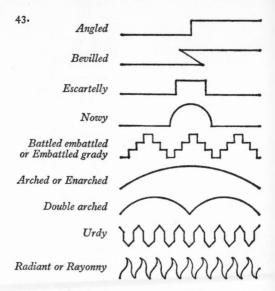

Angled

Bevilled

Escartelly

Nowy

Battled embattled
or Embattled grady

Arched or Enarched

Double arched

Urdy

Radiant or Rayonny

described. We have already demonstrated this in the case of the mullet above. First the field was described, then the principal charge. The charge may be an ordinary, a sub-ordinary or a miscellaneous charge. If its position is not specified it will be assumed to be placed centrally on the field, and also to face the dexter if it is something which "faces" in one direction or another. *Or a lion rampant Gules* means that the red lion is centrally placed on the gold shield, and that it faces towards the left.

44. *Counterchanging.* 45. *Per pale and barry*
Arms of Chaucer

4. *The other charges are described in their order of importance.* Their situation and tincture are always given.

5. *Describe charges which are on charges.* A lion, for example, may in turn be charged with a crescent.

6. *Describe any "differences".* This includes cadency marks such as labels, crescents, and so on.

7. *Overall charges are described last.* Sometimes a charge is placed "overall" on the shield with its charges—perhaps a bordure, or a baton or some such item.

The rule "from top to bottom and from left to right" applies in heraldry. Thus *Per fess Argent and Azure* means that the top is argent and the bottom is azure. *Per pale Gules and Or* means the left side is red and the right side is gold.

Quarters are numbered top left, top right, bottom

left and bottom right, as are quarters within quarters (grand quarters counter-quartered). Gyronny fields are numbered clockwise beginning with the top left hand segment or gyron. The number of gyrons in a gyronny is stated—e.g., Gyronny of eight, Sable and Or.

When several figures appear on the shield, first their attitude and secondly their position must be described. Sir Thomas Innes of Learney gives a classic example in *Scots Heraldry* when he points out the fundamental difference between:

(*a*) three swords in fess paleways; and

(*b*) three swords paleways in fess.

In the first instance the swords are in a fess-like attitude, i.e., horizontal, and are arranged "paleways" one above the other. In the second the attitude of the swords is paleways, i.e., upright, and they are arranged "in fess" so that they run across the centre of the shield.

In practice it is not usual to mention the same colour, metal or fur more than once. When a colour is referred to more than once it is simply described as being "of the first" or "of the second", depending on which was the first, second and subsequent metal, colour or fur mentioned in the blazon.

When blazoning an achievement we do not stop short with the shield. Having described it, the blazon goes on to describe the rest of the achievement, and in the case of Fig. 6, page 17 the full blazon is as follows:

Per fess, Vert and Gules, a boar's head erased

Argent, langued Gules, holding in his mouth the shankbone of a deer proper, in chief: and in base two wings conjoined in lure reversed Argent. Above the shield is placed an Helm befitting his degree with a Mantling Vert doubled Argent, and on a Wreath of the Liveries is set for Crest a hand proper holding a Celtic cross paleways, Or, and in an Escrol over the same the motto l'Audace.

This is quite a simple coat and a short blazon. Much can be learned from an hour or two with a peerage where all sorts of blazons are to be found. For example, the sinister supporter of the arms of the Duke of Atholl is: "A lion rampant Gules, armed and langued Azure, gorged with a plain collar of the last charged with three mullets Argent." Some shields have a shorter blazon than this one supporter!

The basic principles always remain the same. The rules of heraldry can be learned in a day. A week's reading is all that is needed to give anyone a decent working-knowledge of heraldry, from which starting point they can go as far as their time and inclination permit. The sequence of blazoning is absolutely logical. Sometimes a wealth of detail on a shield makes it appear far more complicated than it really is. Once the basic rules are known, it becomes easy to follow even the most lengthy blazon.

CHAPTER IV

THE HONOURABLE ORDINARIES
AND SUB-ORDINARIES

ORDINARIES are the simplest and oldest of the charges and the most important. There are ten of them: the chief, the fess, the pale, the bend, the chevron, the pile, the cross, the saltire, the pairle or pall and the bordure. The bordure, however, although it is an ordinary in the sense that there cannot be more than one on any single shield, is not used as a charge but as a mark of cadency or differencing.

It must be stressed that although some ordinaries, such as the chief, may *appear* like divisions of the field, they are in fact three-dimensional charges which are placed upon the field, and hence the rule of tincture applies. The exception, as mentioned before, is when the field consists of a number of strips, such as barry or bendy, in which case the bars and bends are not charges.

Because the ordinaries are objects placed upon the shield, it follows that they are trimmed to the shape of the shield and therefore those lines which coincide with the edges of the shield will be straight or curved accordingly. Other lines may be either straight or follow one of the patterns in Figs. 40–42, page 48. Taking the chief as an example,

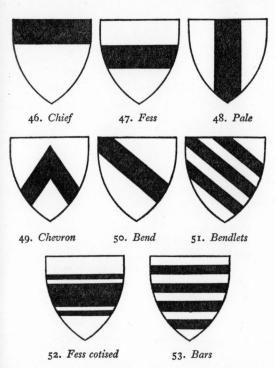

46. *Chief*   47. *Fess*   48. *Pale*

49. *Chevron*   50. *Bend*   51. *Bendlets*

52. *Fess cotised*   53. *Bars*

only the bottom edge could have an irregular outline, such as raguly. The fess may have irregular
lines at the top and bottom, and so on. As a matter of
interest when the fess, chevron or bend are embattled, they are embattled on the top side only;

if they are embattled on both sides, they are described as being embattled counter-embattled.

There can only be one of any ordinary on a shield, but where the ordinary appears in its diminutive form, there may be several. The diminutives are:

chief — comble
fess — bar. The smaller diminutive is the barrulet.
pale — pallet
chevron — chevronel
bend — bendlet. The smaller diminutive is the riband.

There is no diminutive of the pile, but sometimes three piles are displayed in exception to the general rule about the number of ordinaries.

A cotise is a repetition of a charge, having the same outline, with the field appearing in the intervening space. See Fig. 52, page 55.

A chief and a fess each occupy a third of the shield, the chief the upper third and the fess the centre third. Like all ordinaries they can have other charges on top of them. Charges lying on the field in the position normally occupied by a chief or a fess are often described as being "in chief" or "in fess", e.g., Azure a chevron Or, in chief three mullets Argent.

The chief cannot be cotised.

The bar which is the diminutive of the fess is rarely used singly. Fig. 52, page 55 shows two bars and Fig. 54, page 57 shows a field which is a barry of six Argent and Sable. When describing a

54. *Barry*   55. *Baton*   56. *Bend sinister*

57. *Pall*   58. *Cross*   59. *Saltire*

60. *Pile*   61. *Paly*

field barry, paly or bendy, it is essential to specify
the number of bars, pallets or bends, which is
always an even number. The reason for this is
obvious—if you had a barry of *five* Argent and

Sable, you would in fact have Argent two bars Sable! So it must be an even number.

The pale is a vertical band in the centre of the shield, occupying one third of the field, and its diminutive is the pallet which is half the width of a pale.

The bend runs diagonally across the field, issuing from the dexter chief unless it happens to be a bend sinister, in which case it runs in the opposite direction. The diminutive of the bend is the bendlet and the further diminutive is the riband. When the riband is couped or cut short at the ends it is called a *baton*. Sometimes the bendlets are pushed up towards the chief, instead of being centred on the fess point, and when this happens they are said to be enhanced. The arms of Byron are Argent three bendlets enhanced Gules (see Fig. 63, page 59).

The chevron should occupy about a third of the field. In the past the point used to touch the top edge of the shield. Nowadays it is somewhat smaller, to make room for other charges. The diminutive is the chevronel, but a whole field is rarely composed of chevronels.

The pairle or pall is a Y-shaped figure as illustrated (Fig 57, page 57).

The cross is a composite of a pale and a fess. There are so many varieties of cross that it is impossible to list them all, and there is no need to try to memorize them. The student of heraldry soon becomes familiar with the more common varieties— the potent, cross crosslet, paty, moline, fitchy, and so on—but there are over a hundred varieties of

58

62. *Chief indented*   63. *Lord Byron*

the upright cross. The other form of cross is the
saltire, which is composed of a bend and a bend
sinister. It is usually called a St Andrew's cross by
the layman—which is perhaps a little unfair to St
Patrick! The correct description of the Scottish
flag is Azure a saltire Argent, and of Ireland Argent
a saltire Gules.

The bordure is usually placed over all other
charges. Occasionally, however, a chief may be
added to a shield already bordured, as a mark of
honour, and in that case the chief would lie on top
of the bordure which would only show below the
chief.

All of these ordinaries can be divided by lines of
division, just as the field can. Some of the ordinaries can be used in a combination.

In addition to the ordinaries there are thirteen
sub-ordinaries, or as they are more properly called,
subordinate ordinaries. These are:

Canton; Escutcheon; Orle; Tressure; Flanche; Lozenge; Mascle; Rustre; Fusil; Billet; Gyron; Fret; Roundel.

The main difference between an ordinary and a sub-ordinary is that there may be more than one of any particular sub-ordinary on the shield, whereas normally there would only be one of any particular ordinary (except piles, as mentioned).

The roundel appears under a variety of names in heraldry, according to its tincture:

A roundel Argent is a plate

A roundel Or is a bezant

A roundel barry wavy Azure and Argent is a fountain

A roundel Gules is a torteau (Fig. 30, page 43).

A roundel Azure is a hurt

A roundel Vert is a pomme (plural *pomeis*)

A roundel Sable is a pellet

A roundel Purpure is a golpe

A roundel Sanguine is a Guze

A roundel Tenné is, prosaically enough, an orange—which is what it most resembles.

The canton is a small quarter, almost always displayed in the dexter chief, and it always has straight edges. It is usually charged with some other charge (Fig. 30, page 43). Some authorities say that a plain silver canton indicates that the arms have been assumed from a family with which there is no blood connection. In that case it must be a rarity for both the College of Arms in England and the Court of the Lord Lyon in Scotland are reluctant to award any arms incorporating bearings associated with someone with whom there is no blood relationship.

The escutcheon is a shield in the centre of the shield, on the fess point. The arms of Mortimer show an escutcheon Argent, while those of the Hay earls of Erroll in Scotland are Argent three escutcheons Gules. The escutcheon has a special use in England. If a man marries an heiress (that is, a heraldic heiress, not someone who is going to come into a fortune one day) he will display her father's arms on an "escutcheon of pretence", in the centre of his own shield. Their children will be able to quarter the arms. In Scotland the practice is different, and the escutcheon is only used to display the arms of a peeress in her own right on the shield of her husband, and in such a case the escutcheon is ensigned with her coronet of rank.

The orle is simply a bordure which is inside of the shield instead of being coincidental with its outer edge. The tressure is like the orle, but is very narrow and is often shown as a double tressure—i.e., there are two of them close together with the field showing between them. Often a tressure is ornamented with fleurs-de-lis, and it is then described as flory. The arms of the King of Scots are Or a lion rampant within a double-tressure flory counter-flory Gules. In this case the double tressure is ornamented with fleurs-de-lis alternately pointing inwards and outwards. An interesting feature of this is that the stalks of the fleurs-de-lis do *not* show in the gap between the two tressures. The double tressure flory-counter-flory is not normally granted nowadays except in special circumstances.

Flanches are peculiar ornaments almost always shown in pairs, one on each side of the field, and are curved indentations into the field for all the world as though someone had taken a healthy bite out of each side. They reach well in towards the centre.

The lozenge, mascle, rustre and fusil go together. The lozenge is a diamond, and a field covered with lozenges is said to be "lozengy". The mascle is a lozenge voided of the field—i.e., the centre is cut out leaving the field showing. A fusil is an elongated lozenge, which is taller than it is wide. A rustre is a lozenge with a circular hole in the centre through which the field shows. If the tincture showing were not that of the field it would cease to be a rustre and become a lozenge charged with one of the varieties of roundel.

The billet is a small rectangular figure like a brick. If the field is strewn with billets it is called *billette*.

The gyron is one of the segments of the gyronny.

The fret is a mascle with two ribands crossing it in saltire, and they pass over and under each other as illustrated in Fig. 68, page 63. It may cover the whole field, in which case the field is "fretty". The difference between a fretty and a trellis is that when a trellis is charged on a field the bendlets do not pass over and under one another, but instead all the dexter bendlets pass over the sinister bendlets, to which they are nailed. If the nails are of a different

64. *Canton*   65. *Escutcheon*   66. *Flanches*

67. *Gyron*   68. *Fret*   69. *Fretty*

tincture, they are described in the blazon—e.g.,
Or a trellis Vert *cloué* Argent.

Generally speaking, a shield will rarely be charged
only with an ordinary or sub-ordinary, unless it is a
very old coat. Perhaps the most celebrated coat of
arms is that of Scrope, which is Azure a bend Or
(Plate 3). This was the coat over which, from 1385
to 1390, Sir Robert le Grosvenor and Sir Richard
le Scrope invoked the High Court of Chivalry to
decide which of them had the right to bear these
arms. There was actually a third contestant in the
case, a Cornishman called Carminow, not often
mentioned nowadays. The family of Carminow

has died out in the male line, but the arms eventually awarded to them were Azure a bend Or differenced with a canton.

Grosvenor and Scrope are still represented in the male line today, and the real battle was between these two families. Chaucer gave evidence before the court. In the end the arms were awarded to Scrope, and Grosvenor was ordered to difference with a bordure Argent. This he disdained to do, and being highly dissatisfied with the verdict he appealed to Richard II who altered the decision of the court by refusing to allow the bend to Grosvenor *at all*! Grosvenor then adopted a *garb* or sheaf of corn, and the arms Azure a garb Or are to be seen in the first quarter of the arms of his descendant, the Duke of Westminster. As a matter of passing interest, not long ago the Duke of Westminster and Mr Scrope of Danby were both Vice Presidents of the Heraldry Society.

CHAPTER V

MISCELLANEOUS CHARGES

THERE is no end to the number of charges that *can* be devised for use in heraldry, and there is no point in trying to be comprehensive about them. A modern grant of arms might easily include such things as a motor car or an aeroplane. There is no law against it, although it is ultimately left to the discretion of the King of Arms. One thing to bear in mind about such charges is that they date very quickly and whereas a lion passant is the same thing today as it was 400 years ago, and means the same thing to a Spanish heraldist as it does to a Swedish one, a "motor car proper" would mean one thing to an American in the age of the T-model Ford, and yet another to a modern motor racing enthusiast. The herald trying to decide what the arms would look like might easily end up by drawing his own small family saloon!

There is no doubt that some of the most attractive coats are those with simple designs made up from conventional symbols. Even among these conventional charges, however, there are a number of interesting facts governing their use.

First of all, any heraldic object is assumed to be facing the dexter unless otherwise stated. If it is facing the front it is termed "affronté" and if it is facing sinister it is described as "contourné".

One of the best-known charges is the heraldic lion and there are any number of positions in which the lion can be depicted. The lion statant stands facing the dexter, his tail flourishing, and as always his mouth is open and his tongue shows. If one forefoot is raised, he is passant. If he is passant but his head is turned to face the front, he is passant guardant (not affronté, for it is only the head that is turned). If the head is twisted right round so that he is admiring his tail, he is passant reguardant.

A lion rampant is standing on one hindleg, his other legs pawing the air, and in this position he may also be guardant or reguardant depending on the way his head faces. The lion couchant is lying on his stomach, his forelegs stretched out, his hindlegs curled beneath him, his head erect. If he is sitting on his haunches, with his forepaws resting on the ground, he is sejeant. If, however, in this position one forepaw paws the air, he is sejeant erect. In all these positions he may either face dexter, or he may be guardant or reguardant.

When two lions (or any other fierce beasts) face each other they are combatant, and lions are always rampant when combatant. The lion's tail is assumed always to be erect; if it is tucked in between his hindlegs, he is said to be "coward". When the lion is shown about to leap on his prey, rather like the rampant position but with *both* hindpaws on the ground, he is salient. When his head is resting on his forepaws, and he is lying down, he is dormant. Sometimes two lions are shown back to back, and they are then "addorsed". The lion tricorporate consists of one head with three bodies issuing from it in Y or pairle form.

The lion has been mentioned first for it is one of the oldest heraldic charges and was used extensively by sovereigns and nobles of high rank, and appears in the arms of many sovereigns including those of Norway, Denmark, England and Scotland. Many of the expressions which describe lions also describe other heraldic beasts, but there are variations. A stag is never statant guardant, but is "at gaze". A griffin is not rampant but segreant. A stag passant is trippant; and a dog, stag or horse, when running, is courant.

70. *Lion statant*   71. *Lion passant*   72. *Lion rampant*

73. *Lion rampant guardant*   74. *Lion rampant reguardant*   75. *Lion double-headed and coward*

When the head of an animal is displayed itself it is either couped (if it is cut off cleanly at the neck) or erased (if it is torn off raggedly). If it is affronté, however, and no neck shows, it is cabossed, except that if it is a lion's or a leopard's head, it is called simply a "face" and if it is a fox, a "mask". In other words a stag's head cabossed, a lion's face, and a fox's mask are all heads facing the front, with no neck showing.

Animals are said to be "armed" if their claws and horns are of some special colour, but in the case of the stag he is said to be "attired of" his horns if they are of a different tincture. For example, *A stag proper attired Azure*.

Other similar expressions to describe portions specially tinctured are "langued" referring to the tongue, and "unguled" referring to hooves. Thus we might have a unicorn Argent which is langued Gules, armed Or, and unguled Azure—red tongue, gold horn and blue hooves. If an animal's hair is mentioned, it is said to be "crined" unless it has a mane in which case it is "maned". Crined also refers to a man's beard. The boar's head is a very common charge and when its tusks are described it is said to be, e.g., "tusked Or".

Sometimes there is confusion over the heraldic leopard, the question being—When is a leopard not a leopard? There is a theory that the lion and leopard were the same thing, and that they were named entirely depending on their attitude—thus if the animal was passant guardant it was a leopard, but when rampant it was a lion. Certainly the lions of England—and they *are* lions—are passant guardant and they were anciently known as leopards, a name which tended to be used right up to the beginning of the nineteenth century. Nowadays a leopard is the genuine spotted article and quite unmistakable. Some people still speak, wrongly, of the leopards of

England, but it does no great harm as it is an ancient expression and everybody knows what it means.

Among the more interesting heraldic beasts are the mythical ones, and the monsters. There are a lot of them, the dragon being the best known with its scaled body, pointed tail and tongue, and its wings and sharp claws. The griffin is an eagle in front and a lion behind; the female has wings and the male has none. The wyvern is similar to the dragon but has no rear legs, and the cockatrice is exactly like the wyvern except that it has a cock's head instead of a dragon's and also has spurs on its forelegs. The basilisk is a wyvern with a dragon's head on the end of its tail!

The heraldic tiger is a mythical beast, quite unlike a real tiger which is described in heraldry as a Bengal tiger. The ordinary tiger has no stripes, has a horn protruding from its nose, has tusks like a boar and a tufted mane, and has a lion's tail instead of a tiger's. Sometimes it is given the face of a bearded man with two straight horns growing from his forehead, and is then known as a mantygre.

The hydra is obviously many-headed, usually a seven-headed dragon.

There are other monstrous animals such as the opinicus, the sea bear, sea wolf, and sea dog and several others, all rather rare. The most nightmarish of all is probably the Enfield which is composed of the head of a fox, the chest of an elephant, the mane of a horse, the forelegs of an eagle, the body of a greyhound and the tail of a lion. According to L. G. Pine, it is the crest of O'Kelly.

The unicorn, the supporter of the arms of the King of the Scots and also one of the supporters of the present Royal arms, is a horse with a straight horn growing from its forehead (Plates 1 and 2). A unicorn's horn was popularly supposed to have miraculous properties.

A fairly common animal in heraldry is the Agnus Dei, which is a lamb bearing a cross on a banner, and having a halo or nimbus above its head.

When any heraldic animal has a collar or other charge, such as a chain, round its neck, it is said to be "gorged" by whatever the charge is.

There are two positions common to heraldic fish. In the swimming position the fish is said to be naiant; when it is in the palewise position, head upwards, it is said to be hauriant.

Birds are plentiful in heraldry, the best known being the eagle which in the bird world is the counterpart of the lion. It is particularly common in Germanic heraldry, especially when "displayed", i.e., in an affronté position with its wings displayed outwards, tips upwards. When the wings point downwards they are called "inverted". The heraldic eagle displayed is often shown double-headed, the two heads facing in opposite directions (Fig. 78, page 79). Like animals, birds are said to be armed if their beaks and claws are of a special tincture.

A bird very common in English heraldry is the martlet which is a mythical bird like a martin or swallow but usually without any legs. It is one of the marks of cadency, signifying a fourth son, but is also equally often shown as an ordinary charge.

PLATE 1
The Royal Arms
(Reproduced by permission of the Controller,
Her Majesty's Stationery Office)

PLATE 2
The Arms of Scotland

PLATE 3
Some Ancient
Shields of Arms
1. Scrope
2. Montagu (or Montacute)
3. Bardolf
4. Berkeley
5. Willoughby
6. Le Strange

PLATE 4
(*above*) The Royal Arms of England,
Richard I
(*below*) The Arms of H.R.H. Charles,
Prince of Wales

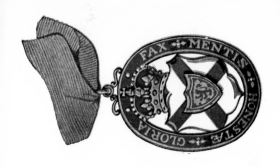

PLATE 5
(*left*) Badge of a
Baronet of the
United Kingdom
(*right*) Badge of a
Baronet of Nova
Scotia

ETON

HAILEYBURY

PLATE 6

(*above*) Arms of Eton College, granted 1449
(*below*) Arms of Haileybury College,
granted 1920

PLATE 7

(*left*) Arms of an Archbishop of Canterbury: the Archbishop's personal Arms are impaled by the Arms of the See of Canterbury

(*right*) Arms of a Cardinal of the Roman Catholic Church: the Cardinal's personal Arms are impaled by those of the See of Westminster

PLATE 8

Heraldic Badges

United Kingdom, Scotland, Ireland, Wales,
Heir Apparent, Portcullis of the Tudors

PLATE 9

(*above, left*) Arms of an unmarried woman
(*above, right*) Arms of a widow
(*below*) Arms of a Peeress in her own right

NISI DOMINUS FRUSTRA

PLATE 10
Impaled Arms of a Husband and Wife

A CLEAN HEART AND A CHEERFUL SPIRIT

PLATE 11
Quartered Arms with two crests

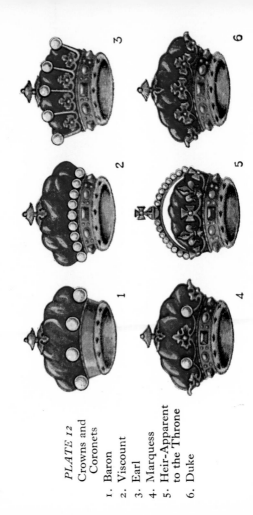

PLATE 12
Crowns and
Coronets
1. Baron
2. Viscount
3. Earl
4. Marquess
5. Heir-Apparent
to the Throne
6. Duke

The arms described in the fourteenth-century Luterell Psalter as belonging to Sir Geoffrey Luterell are *Azure a bend between six martlets Argent.* When the feathers of any bird are trimmed at the edges with any tincture different from the rest of the bird, its feathers are said to be "decked of" the tincture.

When a bird is flying it is volant, and when it is on the ground with its wings drawn in it is close. Birds which do not have talons and bills to rend their prey, are not said to be armed, but to be "beaked and membered". In other words, a dove would not be "armed Gules" but "beaked and membered Gules". The pelican is often shown as wounding its breast and feeding its young with its blood. It is then described as a pelican "in her piety" or as a pelican "vulning herself". This is, of course, quite a mythical idea for the pelican does nothing so far-fetched as to feed its young on its lifeblood. In order to lend some semblance to this myth, the pelican is usually shown with a beak rather like an eagle's. A real pelican's beak would be no use for "vulning".

The phoenix is a mythical bird always depicted as issuing from flames (the salamander is another creature always shown in flames). The harpy is a monstrous bird which is a vulture with the face and breast of a woman.

Turning to inanimate miscellaneous charges, there are special expressions in connection with these too. A five-pointed star with straight edges is called a mullet; when the edges are wavy it is an estoile. A very common charge is an oyster shell, termed an escallop. It was used as a badge by palmers on their way to and from Palestine, and no doubt its frequent occurrence in English heraldry is connected in some measure with the crusades. The escallop is to be seen in the 2nd and 3rd quarters of the arms of Sir Winston Churchill (Fig. 3, page 7).

A tree uprooted is said to be eradicated. If the brickwork of a castle or tower is outlined by lines of a contrasting tincture, it is said to be masoned— e.g., *Azure a castle triple-towered and embattled Argent, masoned Sable, windows and portcullis Gules.*

A sheaf of corn is always called a garb. A rose in heraldry is a five-petalled one, and the five leaves and the seeds are often of different tinctures; e.g., *A rose Gules barbed and seeded proper.* A rose ensigned by a crown is the badge of the servants of the English monarch, and the rose is frequently met with in military heraldry. When barbed and seeded "proper" the barbs or leaves are green and the seeds yellow. Otherwise the barbs and seeds must have their tincture stated.

The cinquefoil is a five-petalled leaf. There is also a trefoil (three petalled) and a quatrefoil (four petalled). When a leaf is shown with its stalk it is said to be "slipped". A trefoil is *always* slipped; quatrefoils and cinquefoils are *never* slipped.

A charge very common in Scotland, particularly among the clans of the Western highland seaboard, is the lymphad or heraldic galley. It was an ancient one-masted oar-propelled ship, usually shown as flagged at both ends and at the topmast. The earldom of Arran has as its arms *Argent a lymphad with sails furled proper, flagged Gules*. The 3rd quarter of MacKinnon of MacKinnon is *Or lymphad, sails furled, the oars saltirewise Sable, flags flying Gules*. When the oars are in the water they are sometimes described as *oars in action* (MacDonald of MacDonald, Lord MacDonald, Lyon Register XXXV, 44).

There are several crowns used in heraldry other than the coronets of rank of peers. There is the mural crown which is embattled and masoned, and is usually only granted to distinguished soldiers. The naval crown, now exclusively reserved for admirals, is composed of sails and sterns of ships (see page 115). A more recent design is the astral crown, composed of wings and stars, used in grants to distinguished leaders of the Royal Air Force. The antique crown is a simple metal circled with tall spikes, and when each spike is topped with a star it becomes a celestial crown.

When arms are granted to clergymen, instead of showing a helmet they display an ecclesiastical hat. A bishop would have a mitre instead. A bishop can impale the arms of his See with his personal arms (Plate 7). When a clergyman is granted arms he does not usually show a crest, but as the arms will pass to his descendants who may not be clergymen, a crest will appear separately in the margin of the patent, for their use with helmet and liveries.

When an ordinary or sub-ordinary is placed over a charge, the charge is said to be debruised by it. When one charge is placed on top of another charge, the first is generally said to be surmounted by the second. When arms are within a bordure, the coat is first described and then is said to be "all within". Thus we get *Argent a chevron between three otter's heads erased Gules, all within a bordure of the last.* But if the bordure went over anything—e.g., if there was a chief, and a bordure on top, then the blazon would end "over all a bordure Vert."

The question of abatements in heraldry is a difficult one. The definition of an abatement is a mark of degradation on the arms. There are a number of conventional marks of abatement. Before considering them, it is essential to make it clear that the baton sinister or any other mark of illegitimacy is not an abatement.

Marks of illegitimacy have no reference to character, but only to succession to property. They cannot therefore be considered as abatements or degradations.

The commonest abatements are the point and

the gore. The point cuts off an angle of the shield, either one of the two top corners, or else the base. It may have straight or curved edges.

Points and gores were supposed to have been awarded for lying, boasting, sloth in war, drunkenness, revoking a challenge, for killing a prisoner who has yielded and for seduction and rape.

It is by no means certain that abatements were ever used. They are certainly mentioned by heraldic writers of a few centuries ago, but there was a whole class of heraldic literature written from the sixteenth to the eighteenth centuries roughly, which was very poor indeed mainly because the writers refused to see heraldry as a practical science, and invested it with all sorts of meanings of their own which had no real basis in fact. Many of these wrong ideas still exist. It is from this period of bad heraldry that references to abatements are usually drawn, and therefore the books in which they appear are pretty useless as evidence.

The arguments against abatements ever having existed is that arms are honourable symbols granted by the Crown, and that marring the shield with so-called marks of disapproval—abatements of the individual's honour—is foreign to the whole purpose of heraldry. We should perhaps qualify this a little by saying that arms fundamentally were and are for identification, and purely secondarily have developed into symbols of honour. The knight of old who blotted his escutcheon was unlikely to receive a letter from the College of Heralds saying that the King had awarded him a *Gore sinister*

Tenné for being tipsy at the last Wappenschaw, and would he please have it put on his shield without delay. Apart from the unlikelihood of the whole thing, it is even less likely that the good knight would trouble to comply!

For any really drastic offence, such as High Treason which was regarded as much more fundamentally terrible than a night on the malmsey or chasing a few maidens round the battlements, the arms were reversed and destroyed in some public place by the heralds. In Scotland this was done at the Mercat Cross in Edinburgh. Even so it was rather a waste of time as the nobility were forfeit one year and back in favour and power again a few years later. Some must have had their arms trampled and torn several times in the course of a tempestuous career.

The arguments in favour of abatements are rather weak. Certainly the stock argument that you cannot have good conduct marks without corresponding bad conduct marks is sheer nonsense since arms are not and never have been good conduct marks. If we go back to the origins of heraldry, when it was simply a matter of identification in peace and war by people who had cause and need to identify themselves, abatements would not and could not have had any purpose.

Before leaving the question of the charges, we must take note of canting arms, which are very ancient in their origin, and remain popular today. Canting arms are arms which are allusive to the name of the bearer—rather like a heraldic pun

77. *Bowes*

(see Fig. 77)! For example the heraldic name for whirlpools is gorges, and a medieval family named Gorges bore a whirlpool as its arms. There are many examples of this. Shakespeare's arms show a spear (see Fig. 89, page 99); Lord Crook of Carshalton has a shepherd's crook. People called Pike display a pike, and people called Lucy display a luce which is another fish. Escallops are used by Shelleys and Palmers. There is no end to it—a cock for Mr Fowler, a barry field for someone called Barry and so on.

Generally speaking the applicant for a grant of arms will be advised by the Kings of Arms, and although his preferences will be given full weight, the final decision lies with them. They normally go to a lot of trouble to please an applicant and their advice is invaluable.

CHAPTER VI

ARMOUR AND HERALDRY

THIS is not a book about armour, which is a highly specialized subject, but heraldry is concerned to some extent with armour since the shield and helmet are actual components of an armour. By the end of the first century some of the finest armour was being made and at this time heraldry was flourishing. This armour is quite different from that of, say, 1100 when the hauberk was the principal protection in battle.

The hauberk was a garment of mail (often called chain mail) which covered the wearer from neck to knee. It had a hood which was pulled up over the head. The head was protected below the mail by a padded cap called an arming cap, and on top of the mail was placed a small conical helmet. The mail harness left the face of the wearer exposed. This was the general type of armour worn up till about 1300, when the effectiveness of the halberd and the longbow made mail useless and plate became popular.

From the point of view of heraldry it is the helmet that interests us most, since there is greater variation in helmets than shields. From the open-faced mail coif with its arming pad and conical steel headpiece, the development was to a helmet with a face-piece

78. *Imperial eagle, at King's Langley*

or visor. Thus evolved the bascinet with its movable visor which could be raised or dropped and which afforded complete protection for the face.

The bascinet had a curtain or mantle of mail hanging from its lower edges to protect the neck and chin. This was the type of helmet in popular use up to the early part of the fifteenth century when it gave way to a solid helmet without any mail curtain or "aventail". The great bascinet, as it was called, was all plate and was the forerunner of the close helmet of the next century. Also about this time, early in the fifteenth century, the armet appeared, and this also gave complete protection to the face. A great many of the helmets used in the achievements of knights and baronets, which are usually open-visored, are armets.

There is another type of helmet, however, which we have mentioned before—the helm. This was not part of the basic armour, but an extra accessory, and was probably only worn in tournament. The effigy of Ritten von Steinberg in St Martin's Church, Hildesheim, shows the fourteenth-century knight wearing a bascinet with mail aventail, and carrying a crested great helm. The great helm is sometimes called the pot helm. It rested on the top of the head, and was unwieldy and insecure, as well as heavy and uncomfortable. It was kept in place by laces fastened inside.

The tilting helm did not come into vogue until about the mid-fifteenth century. This is sometimes referred to as the frog-mouthed helm because of its shape and design. It was useless for anything else but the tilt. It was impossible to see out of it unless the head was bent forwards as it would be when running a course. It was very much safer in the tilt-yard than the pot helm with its central eyepiece through which a splintered spear could penetrate.

Strictly speaking, the great helm and the tilting helm ought not to be allowed to esquires and gentlemen, since they were only worn by persons of tournament rank which appears to have been synon-

79. *Bascinet from Black Prince's effigy*

80

ymous with knighthood. This is, however, a technicality, and these helms are used today in official grants to esquires and gentlemen who, in any case, are not supposed to have an open visor and for whom the great helm or tilting helm is particularly convenient. There is at long last a welcome tendency to use this type of helm for knights and baronets too, who would certainly possess them.

There were other types of helmet—and as this is not a technical book about armour I am using the word "helmet" in its general heraldic sense and not in any precise way. Among them were the sallet, the burgonet, the barbute and the morion. None of these, however, is likely to be seen on a heraldic achievement.

The shield was generally "shield-shaped" or, as it is often termed, "heater-shaped". It was fitted with several straps inside, some small ones for the arm and hand, and a larger one—the *guige*—for hanging round the neck. When not being worn, the shield was generally suspended from some convenient peg, and usually hung aslant. This is the reason why nowadays heraldic artists often show the shield in the *couché* or aslant position, which is much more realistic than balancing on its point. Even so a good many people don't like it, perhaps feeling that it looks as though their shield is falling down. The individual can please himself how he shows his shield. An armet or bascinet would be more than half the size of the shield, which was really quite small and manageable. The great helm or jousting helm would be almost the same size as the shield.

There was an attempt to revive the splendour of the tournament in the last century when, in 1839, Lord Eglintoun held a full-scale out-of-doors tournament at Eglintoun Castle in Scotland. The month was August. It was a complete and remarkable re-creation of the real thing, with a Queen of Beauty, pavilions each carrying the banner of the occupying knight, shields on display so that challenges might be registered, heralds, pursuivants and judges in attendance and so on. The show of armour was unparalleled and no expense was spared to re-create the authentic tournament setting. It must have been an impressive occasion which would live in the memories of all who saw it. It was never repeated. But perhaps there is good reason for this.

It rained!

CHAPTER VII

THE RIGHT TO BEAR ARMS

THE control of heraldry and the granting of armorial bearings is vested in the various offices of arms of which there are three in the British Isles—the College of Arms in London, the Court of the Lord Lyon in Edinburgh, and the Office of the Chief Herald of Ireland in Dublin. Arms in the United Kingdom (which excludes Eire) are granted by the Crown although the sovereign delegates this responsibility. The persons on whom the Royal prerogative devolves are the Kings of Arms.

80. College of Arms

The College of Arms controls heraldry in England. It is situated in Queen Victoria Street, London. It was incorporated in 1484 by Richard III, but was actually founded earlier by Henry V. The head of the College is the Earl Marshal of England, an office which for some considerable time now has been hereditary in the family of the Dukes of Norfolk. The responsibilities of the Earl Marshal are shared by Garter Principal King of Arms, who is the executive head of the College and who acts very much as an assistant to the Earl Marshal. Garter usually deals personally with grants of arms to peers.

Under Garter King are two subordinate Kings of Arms, Clarenceux King of Arms who "rules" south of the River Trent, and Norroy King of Arms who rules north of it. Working under these three kings are the heralds of whom there are six in England—Somerset, Chester, Windsor, Richmond, Lancaster and York. Lastly there are the junior officers of arms, the pursuivants, of whom England has four—Rouge Croix, Rouge Dragon, Portcullis and Blue-mantle. Oddly enough the offices of Clarenceux and Norroy Kings of Arms are older than that of the Garter King whose office came into being sometime after the Most Noble Order of the Garter. From the date of his creation, however, Garter King was given jurisdiction over the two provincial Kings.

There is no College of Arms in Wales, and there are no Welsh heralds. Wales is regarded as being a part of England as far as heraldic control is concerned, and even anciently Welsh arms were dealt with by the English establishment. The Charter of Richard III incorporating the College mentions one, Richard Champney, Gloucester King of Arms 'for Wales". The Welsh do not all accept this state of affairs and many of their great families have refused to register and record arms in England even though they actually use them and have done for centuries. There is, however, much interest in heraldry among the Welsh, just as there is in other parts of the British Isles. There is now a Royal badge for Wales, surmounted by the Royal crown, and which is for use on all Government publications and letter headings used by Welsh departments (Plate 8).

In Scotland the control of heraldry is fully legal, as the Court of the Lord Lyon is part of Scotland's judicature, and the display and use of arms is strictly regulated and protected by Scottish law. The Lord Lyon King of Arms is the chief Officer of Arms in Scotland, and in fact holds the oldest heraldic office in Great Britain, the origins of which are lost in the mists of antiquity. The Lord Lyon is a Great

81. *The Duke of Norfolk, Earl Marshal of England: shield at the College of Arms*

Officer of State and of the Crown, a judge of the realm, and it is high treason to strike or deforce him. His office is pre-heraldic and it combines the very ancient office of Royal Sennachie or Bard, one of the most important and ancient offices in the Royal Household. Lyon is more nearly a counterpart of the Earl Marshal, than the Garter King of Arms, although in fact he has no exact counterpart in England. His office is unique and he has powers, such as those of imprisonment and fine, which no English officer has and which even now he does not hesitate to use.

Like the Earl Marshal, the Lord Lyon is responsible to the sovereign for the arranging of State and public ceremonial, but unlike the Earl Marshal he is personally concerned with all aspects of the practical application of heraldry in Scotland, and is much more involved in the day-to-day work of his heralds and pursuivants than is the Earl Marshal. Under the Lord Lyon there are three Scottish heralds—Albany, Marchmont and Rothesay. The three pursuivants are Carrick, Unicorn and Kintyre.

The position in Ireland was complicated when Eire became an independent republic. Anciently there was an Ireland King of Arms, but he was part of the English establishment and was on one occasion even described as the senior *English* herald! This office was of short duration and in 1553 Edward VI established the office of Ulster King of Arms who was a King of Arms of equal status to the English Kings Clarenceux and Norroy, and whose province was all Ireland. This office remained active until 1940 when Sir Neville Wilkinson, the last Ulster King of Arms, died. For some years, since the founding of the Irish Free State, his office had been something of an anomaly, but as it was a Crown appointment the Government of Eire was hardly in a position to abolish it. Sir Neville Wilkinson became Ulster King before Eire separated from the rest of the United Kingdom, and the office had been granted for life.

After his death the office of Ulster was combined with that of Norroy as far as the six counties of Northern Ireland are concerned. In Eire the Irish Government set up its own heraldic office consisting of the Chief Herald of Ireland and one genealogical officer. The Chief Herald of Ireland deals with the twenty-six counties of Eire and with citizens of Eire who reside in England or in other countries.

86

82. *Garter King of Arms*   83. *Lyon King of Arms*
84. *Ulster King of Arms*

British citizens resident in Eire do not come under him but under the College of Arms or the Court of the Lord Lyon as the case may be.

The general position of persons resident abroad is that they apply to the Office of Arms in the country in which they were born or from which they are claiming descent. Thus the exiled Englishman comes under the jurisdiction of the College of Arms, and the exiled Scot deals with the Lord Lyon.

Citizens of dominion countries apply to the country of their descent. Grants of arms are made every year, in increasing numbers, to citizens of Canada, New Zealand, Australia and other countries as well as to people outside the Commonwealth, such as Americans. The position with regard to Americans is both curious and complicated. One way in which they get round the fact that they are not theoretically eligible for a British grant of arms is to apply in the name of a proved ancestor and once they have got arms for him, to re-apply for arms as his descendant. Of course, if they happen to have an armigerous ancestor already then they simply apply for his arms, differenced if necessary to show cadetship.

When a man changes nationality the position is even more involved. The correct position is to apply for a re-grant of arms by the heraldic authority of the new country, assuming that the new country has one. If it has none, then the right to the arms is lost. For example, if an Englishman casts off his allegiance to the Crown by becoming a naturalized citizen of the United States, then he should cease

85. *Northern Ireland*

to use those marks of honour granted to or confirmed to him as a liege subject of the British Crown. But in fact he will no doubt continue to use his arms although there is no heraldic authority in America where he can re-register them. Ancestral arms, once granted, are not lightly surrendered.

The duties of heralds go back before the days of heraldry—which was originally called armory. Heralds acted as Royal messengers, emissaries and ambassadors, and were employed in time of battle to convey messages from one princely commander to his opponent. There is a curious idea that heralds carried trumpets. Nothing could be further from the truth. They were persons of considerable consequence, and were sometimes accompanied on their missions by a trumpeter who blew his trumpet to achieve silence and attention for the herald, particularly when he was charged with the duty of

89

making any sort of public proclamation on the King's behalf.

Heralds had many other duties, which included the reckoning-up of the dead in battle (not the most pleasant part of their job), the control and regulation of ceremonial at tournaments, and the supervision of the funerals of the nobility. Obviously as hereditary symbols were adopted, and the science of armory came into existence, it was the heralds who would become most familiar with the various coats of arms worn by the nobility of their own and other countries. The control of tournament ceremonial must have given the heralds some local and temporary say in armorial affairs, yet in the great *cause célèbre* of the English Court of Chivalry, Scrope v. Grosvenor 1385-1390, no heralds appear in the record, so at that time the ultimate control of such matters did not rest with them. In the case of Scrope the appeal against the verdict of the Court was to the King.

Gradually, however, as the use of arms spread and as the number of appeals to the crown regarding duplication of arms increased, the position was regulated by the King passing over to the heralds the control of armory. And what no doubt began as an "extra job" for the heralds became increasingly important as their other duties died out. Heralds nowadays have few warlike, funereal or ambassadorial tasks to perform, and mercifully do not have to count the dead in time of war, but the regulation and control of arms—what we now call "heraldry" —is very much a full-time job for them.

86. *Eire*

For about a century and a half, from about the mid-sixteenth century till the end of the seventeenth century, the heralds went forth from time to time on visitations for the purpose of recording pedigrees and arms. In England this was the beginning of the genealogical part of the herald's office, but in Scotland genealogy had always been a prime concern of the Lord Lyon. The visitations served several purposes, the most important being that arms actually in use were recorded and entered in public records, along with pedigrees. Much of our present knowledge derives from these visitations. There was no systematic plan of covering the countryside, but most countries were visited more than once and indeed second visitations were generally necessary to give people time to gather the requisite proofs which the heralds had demanded first time round.

Who is entitled to bear arms? The answer is not

simple. In the beginning arms were, beyond any doubt, *assumed*, and without any reference to anybody. In the instance of Scrope v. Grosvenor there is no reason to believe that anyone originally "granted" permission to the Scropes, Grosvenors or Carminows to bear the arms *Azure a bend Or*. All three of them claimed ancient use of their arms. None claimed a right derived from any heraldic authority.

As arms came to be controlled by the Crown, and as they became symbols of nobility which could only emanate from the Crown, the assumption of arms became illegal. By the time of the visitations heraldry had ceased to be a pre-eminently practical thing and a good deal of snobbery had crept in. A lot of people adopted arms and pretended they had always been in use in their family. Part of the job of the heralds on their visitations was to root out this sort of thing. Persons who could prove ancient use of arms were now granted permission to continue to use them. Others had to apply for arms or go without. Many people were forbidden to use arms they had assumed at a recent date.

For a long time in England lawyers and tradesmen were disbarred from the use of arms, and so were doctors and farmers. In the seventeenth century, for instance, lawyers, doctors and teachers were held to be fairly lowly persons. In the beginning it was the *need* to use arms, not the desire to establish oneself in society, that gave rise to the spread of heraldry. By the seventeenth century arms were regarded very differently, and were greatly sought after for all the wrong reasons.

87. *The Royal Society, incorporated 1663:* Argent a quarter of England – *a rare example of the coat of England being granted in its entirety and without difference*

88. *Earl Beatty*

In Scotland conditions were somewhat better than they were in the south, for there was less class distinction in Scotland and more clannishness. The Lord Lyon seems to have granted arms much more widely than the English Kings, and differently. Any person who could maintain a horse and harness (i.e., armour) was eligible, and so were all land-owners no matter how unimportant—indeed, these classes of people were expected to seek a grant of arms if they did not already have properly recorded ones.

The position today is that arms have a dual nature. They are both the honourable sign of nobility, and they are a means of identification. Nobody has an *absolute* right to arms, though cadets and descendants

93

of armigers cannot normally be refused in the same way as a new applicant—i.e., because of their bad character. In England arms are granted to the grantee and his descendants, and all his descendants have a right to the arms, differencing them themselves according to their position in the family. They can do this without anybody's permission provided there is a valid grant of arms. In Scotland the grant is only to the man and his heirs of the body, which is rather different and means that younger sons, for instance, cannot use the arms at all until they have applied to the Lord Lyon who will devise a suitably differenced coat. Only then can they display arms. Even so, in Scotland Lyon can hardly refuse a younger son in the same way as he could refuse a new applicant.

It is the case of the new man that gives rise to questions. All public persons and professional men are at liberty to apply for arms and will almost certainly be granted them—and this includes doctors, lawyers and teachers nowadays. The same applies to all regular officers of the Army, Navy and R.A.F., and may well be argued as applicable to temporary officers on the basis that any man who has received his King's or Queen's commission is entitled to the further recognition of arms. A grant may be refused, however, if there is any reason for deeming the applicant not worthy, and there is no appeal against such a decision. Needless to say, once arms are granted, the individual can be as "discreditable" as he pleases. Part of the reason for this is that a person has only a life-interest in his arms once they are granted, and they belong equally to his successors.

The grant of arms to William Shakespeare was criticized at the time it was made on the grounds that he was not a worthy person. Here we have an example of pure social fashion. In Shakespeare's time playwrights and players were persons of no account, generally believed to be disreputable. Today chivalric honours are granted to film stars, and to footballers. Heraldry must survive fashion if it is to survive at all. Nobody nowadays would dream of questioning a grant of arms to Shakespeare.

What happens if Joe Bloggs the dustman applies for arms? The real answer is that he doesn't, but let us consider the matter and assume that he does. Provided that no good cause can be given to the contrary, he would in all probability receive a grant. There is, of course, no real incentive to Joe Bloggs to apply for arms while he is still a dustman, or a roadsweeper, because it is hardly worth getting an illuminated parchment to hang on the wall which will describe his occupation. It is nothing to be ashamed of, needless to say—no honest labour is a matter for shame. But it is rather when Councillor Bloggs begins to think of his descendants that he will think of a coat of arms. Whereas he might not think being a dustman was anything worth writing home about, he quite probably would want to provide a permanent reminder of his position as councillor, and feel that he was a sufficiently distinguished ancestor for his descendants to cite when bringing their title to the arms up to date.

As a most distinguished armorist has said, any person who claims to be a gentleman should not be afraid to make good his claim by the patent of arms which establishes that the Crown accepts him and his heirs as such.

Once arms are granted in England, all descendants share in them. They ought to make up progress of the title to the arms by recording each generation of descent from the original grant. This involves only a very small fee. And if two or three generations forget to make up progress of the title, one can do it quite simply by paying for two or three entries instead of one. It is not wise to let matters get too far out of hand in case the position arises when proof is difficult and it may then be expensive and even impossible to establish a right that need never have been lost in the first place.

In Scotland all younger sons must apply for differenced versions of their father's arms before they have any right to display arms. Eldest sons matriculate the undifferenced arms as they pass to them.

Technically any person in England who uses arms without having had the pedigree made up to date and paid the small registration fee, is wrong. *Legally* in Scotland anyone who uses arms, other than heirs, wives, and daughters who have a courtesy use, who has not matriculated the arms in Lyon court, is committing a crime and at the very least is defrauding H.M. Treasury! They will certainly be fined if they persist, and property may be confiscated.

There is a peculiar situation in Ireland where arms that can be proved to have been used for three generations and for one hundred years will be confirmed. Confirmation is by letters patent and Norroy inherited from the old office of Ulster this power to confirm arms on *proof of user*. This jurisdiction applies only to the six counties of Northern Ireland.

Outside Scotland the legal position is obscure. There can be no official or authorised arms except those which are recorded in the College of Arms, but there is no really effective means of preventing anyone either from devising a coat of arms of their own and using it ("bogus" arms) or from using somebody else's arms ("usurping" arms). When it is considered that a new grant of arms in England costs about £100 and that a grant with supporters may cost as much as £200 (in Scotland the cost is about half and in Ireland even less), one can see that with no effective legislation against offenders, there is both the temptation and the means of defrauding. In England it is the College that is defrauded, not the Treasury.

It is very wrong to use bogus arms, or to usurp somebody else's arms, but it is not punishable in any way except in Scotland.

In 1954 the Court of Chivalry, which had been in abeyance for over 200 years, was revived to deal with a complaint by Manchester Corporation that a music hall had been using the Corporation's arms on the curtain of the theatre, and also on its official seal.

This Court can be traced back to Norman times, and it is pre-heraldic, its original purpose being to deal with military matters and disputes affecting dignity and honour. It was in early times presided over by the Lord High Constable and the Earl Marshal. In heraldic times, of course, it was the obvious judicature for hearing disputes concerning arms.

In 1521 the office of Lord High Constable was abolished and the court went into a decline. By the early eighteenth century it was not in existence, and indeed it was very much doubted if it could ever be revived in practice.

Revived it was, however, in 1954 which was a notable year in English heraldry. Judgment was given against the music hall, not on the grounds that the arms of Manchester Corporation had been displayed on their drop curtain—for there is nothing wrong with this provided the arms are not being "passed off" as belonging to someone else—but for using them on the music hall company's seal, which was a very clear case of usurpation.

It was a momentous step, the convening of the Court, but it is rather doubtful if its protection could be invoked by a private individual. Obviously it is a fantastically expensive piece of machinery. In Scotland the position differs because a court is in daily session dealing with all matters coming under the notice of the Lord Lyon. It is simple for any person who thinks he has suffered injury to obtain a hearing.

The theoretical position is that the Court of

89. *Shakespeare*

Chivalry in England is still operative and that the
laws and rules of heraldry can be enforced by law.
The practical position is much less rosy than one
might think, and it will be extremely interesting to
see when this Court sits again.

If an Englishman applies for and is officially
granted a coat of arms, or has the arms of an ancestor confirmed to him, and he finds someone else
making free with them on a seal or passing them off
in any other way, there is little he can do except to
complain to the other man who, as matters stand,
is quite likely to ignore him.

CHAPTER VIII

CADENCY—HERALDRY IN THE FAMILY

Marks of cadency are used in heraldry to distinguish (*a*) between brothers; (*b*) between the descendants of various brothers.

In England, as already shown, the destination of the grant is very wide. If we take the case of a man who is granted arms *Azure a bend Ermine*, and he has four sons, and each of these four sons has in turn four sons, we have immediately twenty descendants of the original grantee all entitled, in England at any rate, to display and use the arms *Azure a bend Ermine*. If they did so, the result would be utter confusion, and the purpose of heraldry—identification of the individual—would be lost. For this reason there are various marks which are placed on the shield to show whether the bearer of the arms is head of the family, or a second son, or the third son of a fifth son, and so on.

Cadency marks may be either *personal* marks or *house* marks. For example, the second son differences with a crescent, and this is a personal mark to distinguish him from his brothers. The sons of the second son, however, will display the crescent as a *house mark*, and add other marks showing their own position within their house. The eldest son of the second son would thus have a crescent charged with a label, until such time as his father died and he could drop the label.

Figure 90 shows the marks of cadency which are used in England, and these are assumed by people without any reference to the College of Heralds. The three-point label is the cadency mark of the first heir; the second heir (who is the eldest son of the eldest son) uses a five point label. It follows from this that the label, being the sign of the heir to the arms of the head of the house is always a temporary and personal mark, and never becomes a permanent or house mark.

This system looks adequate at first glance, but difficulty quickly arises when the head of the chief house in the family group dies. The eldest son had a label which he now drops. He succeeds to Azure a bend Ermine. His brother, the second son, had a crescent and he retains this as he is still the second son of the late head of the family. But what of the eldest son's own family, if he is married? *His* eldest son had a five-point label which now he discards in favour of a three-point one to show that he is next in line of succession to Azure a bend Ermine. But the *second* son of the new head of the family, who formerly had a label charged with a crescent to show he was second son of the heir, should now drop the label for he had become instead the second son of the head of the family. In other words he now occupies exactly the same position in relation to his father as his *uncle* does to *his* own late father, and both of them display crescents.

The result is confusion. There is no set rule for dealing with this. The Lynch-Robinsons in *Intelligible Heraldry* give a fictitious dialogue at a family conclave designed to resolve this problem, the interesting thing being that the various members of the family sort it out among themselves to their own satisfaction. In Scotland, of course, they cannot do this. Every member of the family must go to the Lord Lyon who, after considering the structure of the family, will assign differences to be born by each descendant of the original grantee. In fact, in England there is nothing to stop people from going to the heralds with their problem and they would receive sensible and sound advice as to how to difference their arms. The fact that they *need* not refer cadency to the heralds does not mean that they *ought not* to do so.

People must difference otherwise heraldry ceases to be useful and becomes merely a matter of having arms of some sort, regardless of the fact that somebody else has them. This is pure snobbery—any old coat of arms for the sake of having it.

The cadency marks used in Scotland are usually bordures, and not martlets, crescents and so on. The label is the only temporary cadency mark used in Scotland and the only one which can be assumed at will by the heir. When his father dies, however, he must go to Lyon Court and have the arms confirmed to him. The younger son who uses his father's undifferenced arms, in Scotland, is usurping the arms, and if he adds a difference of his own contriving, he is using bogus arms. He *must* apply to the Lord

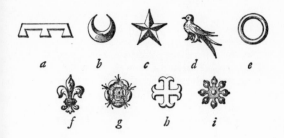

a   *b*   *c*   *d*   *e*

f   *g*   *h*   *i*

90. *Marks of cadency:*

a. *The eldest son (during his father's lifetime), a label*

b. *The second son, a crescent.*

c. *The third son, a molet*

d. *The fourth son, a martlet.*

e. *The fifth son, an annulet*

f. *The sixth son, a fleur-de-lis*

g. *The seventh son, a rose*

h. *The eighth son, a cross moline*

i. *The ninth son, a double quatrefoil, or octofoil*

Lyon for a suitably differenced version of the arms to be matriculated in his name.

This means that no two persons can ever, even by accident, bear the same arms. It is in this very matter of cadency that the difference between Scottish heraldry, and heraldry in many other countries, is strikingly exhibited. Full control of heraldry results in a pure standard, and it is not without reason that Scotland is generally credited with having heraldry in a better and finer form than any other country in the world.

In other European countries there is no complete system of differencing. In Germanic countries, for example, there were many methods of differencing. A common method was differencing by tincture. The Rose group of families, whose charge was a rose, differenced in this way, e.g., Rosenberg used Gules on Argent; Hradec, Or on Argent; Landstein; Argent on Gules; Stráz, Argent on Or, and so on. Other methods were: (1) multiplying figures, e.g., the main family would bear a boar's head and cadet families would bear 2, 3 or 4 boars' heads; (2) differencing by crests, which was a common but not a satisfactory method since the shield is the basis of the arms and the crest is not always displayed; and (3) differencing by inheritance, i.e., by adding inherited charges to the basic shield. In no case, however, was there a clearly formulated and generally used system such as there is in Britain today.

Women do not use cadency marks (Plate 9)— even an heiress presumptive would not use the label since, in theory, her father may yet produce a son who would displace her from the succession. Arms can and do pass to women, but only if there are no sons.

Royalty uses *only* the label as a cadency mark, but it is charged with various symbols to show the position in line of succession to the Crown.

Bastardy marks have varied from time to time. Their purpose is not, as we saw earlier, to cast

91. *Duke of Richmond*   92. *Earl of Munster*

any aspersion on the person bearing them—indeed
in the old days Royal bastards were exceedingly
proud of their parentage and their right to show a
differenced version of the Royal Arms (Figs. 91 and
92). The purpose of such marks was to indicate that
the bearer of the arms was not in legal line of succession to the family estates and honours, or the
undifferenced arms. One interesting point is that occasionally references are still made to a "bar sinister".
A little thought will show that as a bar runs across
the centre of the shield, it cannot be said to be either
dexter or sinister.

The present tendency in England is towards a
bordure wavy rather than a bend or baton sinister,
and in Scotland a bordure *compony* is much used.
There is *no* set rule however, and the King of Arms
has the final say in the matter.

CHAPTER IX

THE ARMS OF A LADY

THE use of arms is not confined to men, nor are they only confirmed to male descendants. A new grant would usually only be made to a man, but thereafter it may descend to women.

First of all, both the wife and the daughters of an armigerous person have a courtesy right to display their husband's or father's arms, and this without any permission from anybody. They do so in a lozenge rather than a shield, and they do not display mantling, crest or helmet. They may, however, show the motto on a scroll. This right is theirs for the duration of their lives, and even when daughters marry they do not lose their right to display their father's arms although, if their husband has arms of his own, it is more customary to impale both coats.

When a man has a daughter and no sons, the arms can descend to her and she can transmit her right in them to her own children. In Scotland she would be granted crest, motto, and also supporters if there were any. A woman in Scotland may also be granted a badge and a standard if she succeeds as a chief or chieftain, or as head of a considerable "following".

When a woman who has a courtesy use of her

father's arms marries a man who himself has arms, they normally impale the arms, without asking anybody's permission. Impaling is done by dividing the shield in two per pale and displaying the husband's arms in the left half of the shield and his wife's in the right half (Plate 10).

If the wife is an heiress and can transmit the arms to her descendants, it is normal in England for her arms to be displayed on an escutcheon of pretence, which is a small shield set in the centre of the husband's shield. The children of the marriage would be able then to quarter the arms of their father with those of their mother but *only*—and this is important—with the permission of the College of Arms who would devise and record the quartered arms (Plate 11). Quartering is one thing in England which must be done through the heralds.

In Scotland the escutcheon of pretence is only used to indicate an heiress who is a peeress in her own right, and an ordinary heiress impales her arms in the same way as a daughter who is not an heiress. The children, however, can apply for quartered arms in just the same way as in England. It should be stressed that where the arms of the wife are only those of courtesy, and she is not an heiress, then she cannot transmit any right to the children of the marriage who inherit only their father's arms.

In England there is no primogeniture among women, so *all* the daughters of a man who has no male heirs, become his heiresses and all succeed equally to his arms, and all can transmit them to their children. Thus several distinct and separate families who have contracted marriage alliances to such daughters may each acquire a quartering which is identical. In Scotland there is only *one* heiress who can transmit the arms. A younger daughter who marries can impale her arms with her husband's, but their children have no right to the mother's.

Where a man has quarterings and marries a woman who is heiress to quartered arms, their children would display all the quarters. It is possible to build up over the centuries a fantastic number of quarters, some people being entitled to display over 300 of them. This is very fine in theory, but in practice it is worse than useless, since such a shield would be impossible to decipher. Quartering is very strictly controlled at the present time, and in Scotland it is not allowed unless it serves some purpose, such as the perpetuation of arms which would otherwise lapse entirely.

When a man has daughters and no sons, he sometimes puts a "name and arms" clause in his will. This stipulates that no one can inherit his arms who does not also accept his name. Sometimes this leads to interesting situations where a husband, on marriage, changes his name to his wife's, so that the arms can descend to their children. There is nothing unnatural in this. There is no law which says that on marriage a woman must take a man's name, it is merely the common custom. What it signifies is that she enters his family. It is equally possible for him to enter her family if it serves any purpose. If she represents an ancient and distin-

93. *De Valence dimidiating*
Claremont-Neslé

94. *Cornwall dimidiating*
De Clare

guished house and he does not, it is logical and
proper for him to keep her family name going. If
he does not do so, the children may still do so by
taking the name of their grandfather.

Sometimes there are interesting "permutations"
of arms, for example, when a bishop who is himself
armigerous marries a wife who has arms. He is
entitled to impale his arms with those of his See,
and also with those of his wife. This is done by
showing two shields. The dexter shield has the
arms of the See in its dexter half and his own arms
in its sinister half; and the sinister shield has his
own arms in the dexter half and his wife's in the
sinister half. Likewise, where a knight of an order
of chivalry impales his arms, he uses two shields—
one has his arms alone surrounded by the circlet
and badge of his order, and the other has his arms
impaling his wife's, usually surrounded by a circlet

of laurel leaves to balance the whole thing. Some very beautiful arrangements can result from this.

In closing, it is interesting to note that the old way of impaling the wife's arms with her husband's was by *dimidiation* which meant that the dexter *half* of the husband's coat was impaled with the sinister *half* of his wife's. This gave rise to some comical results such as when the husband's three lions passant suddenly acquired fishes' tails.

CHAPTER X

HERALDIC DESIGN

THIS has been mentioned already, and there is less to worry about today than there has been for a long time past. Nevertheless, although present day heraldic art work is of an extremely high standard both technically and artistically, the student will see some pretty ghastly specimens without having to look far. One or two fairly standard works which have been kept up to date still have illustrations which would be better taken out altogether.

In the beginning the portrayal of heraldic insignia was remarkably fine. After all, the artist was portraying objects of familiar and almost daily use. The medieval artist knew what a helmet looked like, how large it was, and how it was made and worn. He knew the proportion of helmet to shield, and how the shields hung aslant on their guiges. He saw these things often. Sometimes the artistry was a little crude, but the design was excellent. In the *Armorial de Gelre*, for instance, all the arms are displayed on shields in the *couché* position, the helmets are of good proportion, and oddly and interestingly enough there is no nonsense about closed visors, bars, grilles or the direction in which helmets face. The King of Scots uses an ordinary great helm facing the dexter. The mantling generally hangs straight and unslashed. The crests are as large as the helmet and sometimes larger. Caps of maintenance and crest coronets are shown. A lion may tend to look like a pussy cat, or a boar to resemble a placid pig, but we are obviously looking at a "living art" which is of extreme interest and of pleasant design and arrangement.

Apart from the art work, sometimes the arms themselves are very poor specimens. Those granted to Viscount Nelson and to Lord Kitchener are examples of grants that have nothing to recommend

95. *Lord Nelson*

them. The family arms of Nelson are rather fine, but the admiral was given a chief containing a landscape painting which amongst other horrors displays a palm tree growing in mid-ocean, in defiance of the laws of nature. There are two crests. The sinister one shows the stern of a man-of-war "upon waves". It would be interesting to see how such a crest was worn on a helmet—presumably a washing tub or bird bath would have to be employed.

Kitchener's arms while not so hideously un-heraldic were more reminiscent of a sportsman's blazer badge than the arms of a distinguished English field marshal—crossed flags and a crown with "Khartoum" written on it! In the same tradition, Viscount Gough's arms were so augmented in commemoration of various feats in his military career that the blazon runs into thirty lines of type in the Peerage.

Aeroplanes and ships have been used as armorial bearings in recent times, and Swindon appropriately displays a railway locomotive as the charge on its shield. There is nothing against this, although it may not be long now before railway locomotives, aeroplanes and ships (as we know them) become things of the past, and new and strange craft will replace them. We live in an age of rapid change, and for that very reason most of our modern gadgets do not lend themselves to heraldic use. The point, however, is that modern symbols can be and are used. Perhaps one of the most interesting adaptations of conventional heraldry to ultra-modern purposes is the design of the arms of the United

96. *Helm and crest of Sir Geoffrey Luterell*

Kingdom Atomic Energy Authority which makes use of the pile, among other things, to form a coat that is very aptly allusive and yet which contains no mysterious pieces of unidentifiable scientific apparatus nor a painting of an atomic power station proper! If the Atomic Energy Authority can do it—and they have done it brilliantly—so can others.

The crests used even by ancient families are often disappointing. Clouds, bolts of lightning, arms appearing from nowhere brandishing swords, arrows in flight, the sun in its glory, and other "unsupported" objects which *could not* have been placed on the helmet are used as crests. The crest in its earliest form was probably painted on the helmet or on the metal fan which sometimes rose from the comb of the helmet, but if we look at Sir Geoffrey Luterell's helmet, Fig. 96, we will see that it is the actual arms which are repeated on this

113

fan, not a crest. The old armorials show actual three-dimensional objects, usually moulded in cuirboulli or boiled leather, placed on top of the helmet, and usually secured with a wreath, or, at any rate, the wreath was used to hide the join.

The reason for so many bad crests is that a lot of crests have been added at a much later date to arms which were originally granted without a crest. They were added at a time when helmets were not normally worn, and when people were not concerned with whether or not the crest "made sense". It is for this reason that Nelson's crest of the stern of a Spanish ship on the waves of the sea is so ridiculous.

The crest should be something that could be moulded and fastened to the top of the helmet—which rules out six thunderbolts issuing from a cloud.

The arms of the King of Man in the ancient *Armorial de Gelre* show the interesting crest of a leg upside down, the top of the moulded thigh fitting neatly to the top of the helmet. It towers high above the wearer's head as did many crests. It is an object which, however bizarre, *could* have been worn and undoubtedly *was* worn, which is more than can be said for sun, sea or sky.

The whole subject of design is one of extreme interest, and there is wide latitude in the manner in which arms may be drawn, and the various styles that are permitted. It is for this reason that an achievement may be very bad or very good, depending on who depicted it and when.

The fashions of two centuries ago were mostly

abominable. Those of today are generally extremely beautiful and oddly enough approximate more closely to the original styles as shown in very early illuminations dating from the period when heraldry was in its heyday. Provided the result is both possible and pleasing, nobody is likely to grumble.

97. *Naval Crown, granted as crest coronet to Lord Nelson*

CHAPTER XI

THE PEERAGE IN BRITAIN

PEERS are very much the concern of the Officers of Arms, since all peers are not only eligible for, but are as a matter of *noblesse oblige*, expected to apply for grants of arms. Indeed one could take this further and say that any member of any order of chivalry has a *prima facie* claim to be a "virtuous and well-deserving" person, and would almost certainly be granted arms without demur, and owes it not only to himself but to his order to acquire arms. This applies equally to the fifth class of the Order of the British Empire (M.B.E.) as it does to a Knight of the Garter.

There are many interesting facts about the peerage in Britain.

There are five degrees of peer in Great Britain and they are, in their order of importance, duke, marquis (or marquess—the spelling is optional), earl, viscount and baron (Lord in Scotland, where "baron" has an entirely different meaning). Note that marquess is *not* the wife of a marquis as some people think; the wife of a marquis or marquess is a marchioness.

Not only are there five degrees of peer but there are five types or classes of peerage. There are peers in the peerage of England and Scotland, both created in their respective countries before the Union of Parliaments in 1707. Between 1707 and 1801 all peers created in England and Scotland would be peers of Great Britain. From 1801 onwards all peers in England, Scotland or Ireland would be peers in the peerage of the United Kingdom. Finally Irish peers created before 1801 would be peers in the peerage of Ireland. The five classes are therefore England, Scotland, Ireland, Great Britain and the United Kingdom.

Peers take precedence over other peers in the same rank according to their creation. A viscount in the peerage of England or Scotland would take precedence over one in the peerage of Great Britain who in turn would take precedence over one in the peerage of the United Kingdom.

Most people know that not all peers sit in the House of Lords. All *English* peers do so—provided they are sane, are not minors and are not bankrupt. All peers in the peerage of Great Britain or of the United Kingdom may do so—regardless of whether they are English, Scottish, Irish or Welsh by nationality. Peers in the peerages of Scotland and Ireland, however, are limited to 16 representative peers from Scotland and 28 from Ireland. An Irish peer who is not a representative peer can sit in the House of Commons—but not a Scottish one. The sons of peers can be members of the House of Commons till they succeed to their seat in Lords and this is interesting for, as we shall see, the son of a Marquis may have the title of Earl, and yet may sit in Commons until his father dies when he succeeds to the Marquisate and the seat in the House of Lords. But other Earls, who are in fact peers with the rank of Earl and who have a seat in Lords, may not sit in the Commons.

There are at the present time five Royal dukes, their Royal Highnesses the Duke of Gloucester, the Duke of Kent, the Duke of Windsor, the Duke of Edinburgh and the Duke of Cornwall, Prince of Wales (I have given them in the order of their creation).

Dukes other than Royal dukes are styled "His Grace the Duke of . . .". In direct speech they are addressed either as My Lord Duke or as Your Grace. They and their wives are *never* referred to as "Lord and Lady" but always as the "Duke and Duchess of . . .".

Eldest sons of dukes are born in the *degree* of marquis, but their title depends on their father's second title which may only be that of earl. An eldest son of a duke who is by courtesy an earl would take precedence over all other earls, however, by virtue of his own *degree* being that of marquis. Younger sons of dukes are all known as, e.g., Lord James, Lord Henry, etc., and all daughters are Lady Jane, Lady Emily, and so on. These younger sons *must always* be called by their Christian names.

Let us see how this works in practice. Taking the example of Peter Smith, Duke of Devizes, Marquis of Maidstone, Earl of Exeter and Baron Brandywine, his eldest son would be Marquis of Maidstone, and if he marries and has a son of his own, that son would be Earl of Exeter. The younger sons of the Duke of Devizes will be called Lord Samuel Smith and Lord Joseph Smith, and never under any circumstances Lord Smith. They are younger sons, not peers. In personal address they would be spoken to as Lord Samuel and Lord Joseph.

The duke's daughters retain their title of Lady when they marry. If they marry a peer they share their husband's title, rank and precedence. The daughter of a duke who marries an earl becomes a countess and ranks as such. Her sister who remains unmarried, *or who marries a commoner*, continues to rank as a duke's daughter and goes into dinner before her sister who has married an earl! If Lady Barbara Smith marries Mr Gerald Jones she will be known as Lady Barbara Jones. In other words if the duke's daughter marries into the peerage she exchanges her rank for her husband's and can drop in rank as a result, but if she remains unmarried, or marries outside the peerage, she retains her rank and precedence as a duke's daughter. Incidentally, if a duke's daughter, Lady Emily Smith, marries the younger son of another duke, say Lord Harry Brown, she would call herself Lady Emily Brown, not Lady Harry Brown—the reason is that all peers' daughters rank as *one degree higher* than younger sons in the same grade.

When the duke's younger sons, Lord Samuel and Lord Joseph, marry their wives (unless themselves daughters of dukes) become Lady *Samuel* Smith and Lady *Joseph* Smith. And in speech they are addressed as "Lady Samuel" and "Lady Joseph".

Like a duke, a marquis or marquess—style optional—usually has a lesser title which goes to his eldest son. Like dukes, the titles of marquesses are usually taken from the name of a place, although there are a very few exceptions where the title is taken from the family name (The Marquess Townshend is one). There are also two cases in which although the title is taken from a place, the word "of" is dropped—Marquess Camden and Marquess Douro.

Marquesses are styled The Most Honourable, and are addressed as My Lord Marquess or My Lord. Their eldest sons, like those of dukes, take the highest courtesy title and use it as if it were of right. Younger sons and daughters are in all respects treated as those of dukes—i.e., they are Lord or Lady plus their Christian name.

Earls take their titles either from a place, or from the family name, and sometimes two titles are combined in one person. When the title is territorial the word "of" usually appears, but not always so. Again there are usually subsidiary titles, and the highest is taken by the eldest son. If there is no subsidiary title, he is known as "Lord" followed by his *surname*—e.g., the eldest son of the Countess of Erroll is Lord Hay. Younger sons, however, are not Lords, but Honourables, and there is nothing to distinguish them from the sons of viscounts and barons. The wife of such a younger son is also known as The Honourable—e.g., The Hon. Mrs. James Robinson.

Curiously enough, however, the daughters of earls are not Honourables, but Lady plus their Christian name, like the daughters of marquesses and dukes.

Earls are styled The Right Honourable—so are viscounts and barons. They are addressed in speech as "Lord" and their wives as "Lady", as are all peers except dukes and duchesses.

Viscounts, whether territorial or family, do not use the word "of" in their title except in the case of Scottish viscounts in the peerage of Scotland. For example, Viscount Mersey, and Viscount Hereford, but Viscount *of* Arbuthnott. Their eldest sons, like younger ones, are Honourables, and they carry this title into marriage. There is one peculiarity here— the designations of Mr and Miss are *never* used with Honourable. Thus the Hon. Harold Jones, and the Hon. Felicity Jones; but the Hon. *Mrs.* Harold Jones. Sometimes, for example, the daughter of a viscount marries, say, a baronet, and if she married Sir Charles Smith she would become The Hon. Lady Smith.

Baron is the lowest degree of the peerage, and is in all respects similar to viscount as far as usage is concerned. In England the title "baron" is never used, even though it is the legal term—Baron Brandywine is invariably referred to as Lord Brandywine. In Scotland the legal term is not baron at all, but Lord—Scottish barons are persons possessing feudal baronies, which are frequently much older than peerages, and have nothing to do with them. Thus Sir Thomas Innes of Learney is *Baron Learney*; but not Lord Learney.

Ranking immediately below the peers are the baronets who, like knights, are prefixed by "Sir" but whose title, unlike that of knight, is hereditary. When the title is used it is followed by the suffix "Bt" *not* "Bart" which is strictly said to be wrong. The wife of a baronet, like a knight's wife, is Lady. The children have no titles at all. Baronets augment

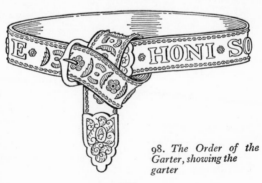

98. *The Order of the Garter, showing the garter*

99. *The Order of the Garter showing the collar*

their arms with either the badge of the Baronets of
Nova Scotia if they are Scottish baronets of this
particular baronetage, or with the badge of the
Baronets of England, Great Britain and the United
Kingdom which is usually called the "Red Hand of
Ulster" although Irish heraldists deny that it is the
Ulster hand because it is a sinister hand not a
dexter one (Plate 5).

Knights either belong to one of the orders of
chivalry or are knights bachelor. The orders of
chivalry are, in their order of importance:

The Most Noble Order of the Garter Founded in
1348, and confined generally to Royalty and peers.
Sometimes a very distinguished commoner is

admitted as a special mark of favour—such as Sir
Winston Churchill, and Sir Anthony Eden before
his elevation to the peerage as Earl of Avon. The
ribbon of the order is blue, and the motto HONI SOIT
QUI MAL Y PENSE is inscribed on the garter itself.
There is a Garter King of Arms who, under the
Earl Marshal, is head of the College of Arms, and
there is an Usher of the Black Rod. It is not generally known that the Prince of Wales is a part of
the Order, and his name is entered on the official list
from the date on which he becomes Prince of Wales,
although some years may elapse before the sovereign

100. *Insignia of the Order of the Thistle*

decides to knight him and invest him with the insignia of the order. See Figs. 98 and 99.

The Most Ancient and Most Noble Order of the Thistle This order was revived in 1687, and is confined to Royalty and to Scottish nobles which includes non-peers, because the noblesse of Scotland comprehends technical commoners. The ribbon of the order is green, and its motto is NEMO ME IMPUNE LACESSIT. The Lord Lyon is its King of Arms and there is an Usher of the Green Rod. (Fig. 100.)

The Most Illustrious Order of St Patrick This order was founded in 1783 and now consists only of Her Majesty the Queen, and the Dukes of

101. *Insignia of the Order of St Patrick*

124

Gloucester and Windsor. Its King of Arms is Norroy and Ulster King of Arms. The ribbon is sky blue and the motto is QUIS SEPARABIT? It has not been conferred since 1934 and is obsolescent.

The foregoing three orders are the most exclusive and the most senior, and the recipients use the letters after their name, thus K.G., K.T., K.P.

The Most Honourable Order of the Bath This is the most important order of chivalry conferred on commoners, and unlike the first three, has more than one class of member. It was founded in 1725, its ribbon is crimson, and its motto is TRIA JUNCTA IN UNO. It has both civil and military divisions. The following are the grades—1st class, Knight Grand Cross (G.C.B.); 2nd class, Knight Commander (K.C.B.); and 3rd class, Companion (C.B.). These three grades exist in both divisions. There is a Bath King of Arms (who is not a member of the College of Arms, and whose duties are confined to his Order), and there is an Usher of the Scarlet Rod. See Figs. 102 and 103.

The Order of Merit This is not an order of knighthood. It is limited to twenty-four members and has two divisions, military and civil. It was instituted in 1902 and its ribbon is blue and crimson. (Fig. 105.)

The Most Exalted Order of the Star of India This order, instituted in 1861, has three classes: Knight Grand Commander (G.C.S.I.), Knight Commander (K.C.S.I.) and Companion (C.S.I.). It has not been conferred since 1947 and is obsolescent. The ribbon is light blue with white edges and the motto is HEAVEN'S LIGHT OUR GUIDE.

The Most Distinguished Order of St Michael and St George Founded in 1818, this is the usual reward for distinguished service in the British Empire and Commonwealth. Its ribbon is saxon blue with a scarlet centre, and its motto AUSPICIUM MELIORIS AEVI. There is a King of Arms and a Gentleman Usher of the Blue Rod. The grades are Knight Grand Cross (G.C.M.G.), Knight Commander (K.C.M.G.) and Companion (C.M.G.). (Fig. 104.)

The Most Eminent Order of the Indian Empire This order, like the Star of India, has not been conferred since India achieved her independence in 1947, and never will be conferred again. There are three grades—Knight Grand Commander (G.C.I.E.), Knight Commander (K.C.I.E.) and Companion (C.I.E.) The ribbon is imperial purple and the motto is IMPERATRICIS AUSPICIIS. The order was founded in 1877.

The Royal Victorian Order. This order is awarded for service to the Royal Family and is frequently bestowed upon Kings of Arms. It was founded in 1896 and has a blue ribbon with red and white edges, and the motto VICTORIA. There are five classes in the order—Knights Grand Cross, Knights Commander, Commanders (C.V.O.), and Members (M.V.O.), the latter being either 4th class or 5th class. Women are admitted to the order, and instead of Knight Commander we get Dame Commander

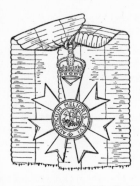

102. *The Order of the Bath Military*

103. *The Order of the Bath Civil*

104. *The Order of St Michael and St George*

105. *The Order of Merit*

(D.C.V.O.). A Dame Grand Cross however would still be G.C.V.O. (Fig. 106.)

The Most Excellent Order of the British Empire. This order was founded in 1917 and the ribbon is rose pink edged with pearl grey. In the military division there is an extra pearl grey stripe in the centre of the ribbon. The order has a King of Arms and a Gentleman Usher of the Purple Rod. There are five classes of member—Knights Grand Cross, Knights Commander, Commanders, (C.B.E.), Officers (O.B.E.) and Members (M.B.E.).

Ranking after the 1st class of the *Order of the British Empire* (G.B.E.), but conferring no title on its limited number of recipients—only sixty-five—is the order of the Companions of Honour founded in 1917, which is open to both sexes. Its ribbon is carmine with gold edges.

Knights Bachelor are knights who do not belong to an order of chivalry, and they rank after Knights Commander of the British Empire. They have a badge worn on the left breast, just like the star of an order of chivalry, and there is an Imperial Society of Knights Bachelor. There is also a baronet's badge worn round the neck, which ranks after the Order of Merit.

The orders of chivalry mentioned above are all British sovereign orders. A British subject cannot accept a foreign order without Royal permission.

Another order which is to be met with in Britain

106. *The Royal Victorian Order*

is the Most Venerable Order of the Hospital of St John of Jerusalem in the British Realm. This is a revival of the Grand Priory in England which was dissolved in 1559, and is to promote charitable work, especially hospital and ambulance work.

The order of precedence of the various insignia of the British orders is as follows:

Victoria Cross

George Cross (both rank above all other insignia)

The Garter

The Thistle

St Patrick

G.C.B.

O.M.

Baronet's badge

The Bath (K.C.D.B., C.B.)

The Star of India (G.C.S.I., K.C.S.I., C.S.I.)

Michael and St George (G.C.M.G., K.C.M.G., C.M.G.)

Indian Empire (G.C.I.E., K.C.I.E., C.I.E.)

Crown of India (C.I.—obsolescent)

Royal Victorian Order (G.C.V.O., K.C.V.O., C.V.O.)

British Empire (G.B.E., K.B.E., C.B.E.)

Companions of Honour (C.H.—comes after G.B.E. and before K.B.E.)

D.S.O.

M.V.O. (class IV)

O.B.E.

I.S.O. (Imperial Service Order)

M.V.O. (class V)

M.B.E.

CHAPTER XII

BADGES, FLAGS, BANNERS AND NATIONAL HERALDRY

THE purpose of a badge in heraldry was for the use of and display by servants, retainers, dependants and followers Such people had often no arms of their own. The display of their lord's arms would have been wrong, so they used his badge. Some examples of well-known badges are the three feathers of the Prince of Wales and the portcullis and rose of Tudor monarchs, as well as the red and white roses of Lancaster and York (Plate 8).

The badge does not form a part of an achievement but is additional to it. Badges are only awarded to people with a considerable following who theoretically have a use for a badge, and they are always awarded with a standard. The badge and standard go together, the one being the personal mark of allegiance and the other the rallying-flag to which the retainers flocked when called out.

The standard does not show the arms but the badge, the motto and the slogan.

One of the commoner errors is that of referring to the Royal arms, displayed in banner form, as the Royal standard. It is in fact a banner, being covered with the actual arms and nothing else. Furthermore, it is used as a banner, only being flown to indicate the Royal presence. A standard did not indicate the presence of the chief or lord; it was the place where his followers rallied and awaited his arrival, accompanied by his banner-bearer.

The national flags are well known—the Union Jack, and the St George's, St Andrew's and St Patrick's crosses. These national flags may be displayed by any patriotic citizen. Often in Scotland people quite wrongly display the banner of the King of the Scots—the red lion on his gold field. Attractive and picturesque as this is, it is not a national flag but a Royal banner. There are a few people who from time to time officially represent the person of Her Majesty in Scotland and who have the power invested in them to display the Queen's Scottish banner on certain occasions. It is rather a pity that a large proportion of the Scottish population also displays it on festive occasions. In fact the public are usurping the Royal Arms and technically are liable to punishment. It would be impracticable for the Lord Lyon to fine half the population of Scotland, but it is perhaps surprising that steps have not been taken to restrain manufacturers from marketing these banners to the public. Anyway it is a well-established custom now and a curiously interesting lapse in a country which has an exemplary heraldic tradition.

Royal arms are different from the arms we have been considering up to now. They are arms of sovereignty. They are not the personal arms of the Royal Family *as a family* but the arms of the monarch of the country regardless of what family happens to enjoy that distinction. In other words, they are the arms of the person who succeeds to the dominions, whatever form the succession might take—whether by simple heredity, or by election or by conquest.

The Royal Arms descend with the sovereignty and the dominions, and unlike other arms in England, the younger children of the sovereign have no right to arms at all until a suitable version has been devised and granted to them by Royal Warrant. Not for Royal princes the right of their subjects to take their father's coat of arms and stick a crescent or a mullet on it as they please.

There are several versions of the Royal arms. There are the Arms of Great Britain as used officially in England (Plate 1), the Arms of Great Britain as used officially in Scotland and the arms of the King of the Scots which are still in use in Scotland (Plate 2). All three versions are perfectly legal and current.

The form of Royal Arms as used in England is

107. *Banner of Sir John Botetourt, temp. Edward I*

108. *Richard II*

109. *Banner of Sir Ralph de Monthermer, as Earl of Gloucester*

quite recent. It was not till the reign of Queen Victoria that the present version came into use. The official blazon is:

Quarterly: 1st and 4th Gules three lions passant guardant in pale, Or (for England); 2nd Or a lion rampant within a double tressure flory counter-flory Gules (for Scotland); 3rd Azure a harp Or, stringed Argent (for Ireland). The whole is encircled with the garter, the principal English order of chivalry. The supporters are dexter a lion rampant guardant imperially crowned Or, and sinister a unicorn Argent, armed, crined and unguled Or, gorged with a coronet composed of crosses patés and fleurs-de-lis, a chain affixed passing between the forelegs and reflexed over the back, all gold.

It was about the reign of Richard I, near the end of the twelfth century, that the King of England began to use a shield Gules, three lions passant guardant Or (Plate 4). About 150 years later Edward III quartered this with the lillies of France not, as one might naturally suppose, with France in the 2nd and 3rd quarters but with France 1st and 4th, England being 2nd and 3rd.

At the beginning of the fifteenth century the field of semé of lilies was changed to Azure three fleurs-de-lis Or, still representing France, and the arms of England remained thus till the time of the Union of the Crowns in 1603, when James VI of Scotland ascended the English throne as James I of Great Britain. At this accession the arms of Scotland and Ireland were added and the coat became 1st and 4th grand quarters counter-quartered 1st and 4th France, 2nd and 3rd England; 2nd grandquarter Scotland; 3rd grandquarter Ireland.

In 1707 the Treaty of Union between Scotland and England gave Queen Anne a brief to approve new arms and on 17th April, 1707, the arms became Quarterly: 1st and 4th England and Scotland per

110. *The Royal Arms, 1340–c. 1400*

111. *The Royal Arms, c. 1400–1603*

112. *The Royal Arms, 1603–88*

pale; 2nd France; 3rd Ireland. The claim to France had not yet been relinquished.

When the House of Hanover came to the throne in 1714 they naturally brought their arms with them which they placed in the 4th quarter, and in 1801 the whole thing was altered again: France was dropped completely, and the arms were Quarterly, 1st and 4th England, 2nd Scotland, 3rd Ireland, and overall in an escutcheon of pretence, Hanover ensigned with an electoral bonnet. In 1816 the bonnet became a crown.

On the accession of Queen Victoria the arms of Hanover, which had passed to the Duke of Cumberland, were dropped altogether and the present arrangement was finally reached.

This chopping and changing was as nothing compared with the change of supporters. These came into use about the time of Richard II who modestly had his shield supported by two angels and under it was a white hart couchant, gorged and chained Or. Henry IV got rid of the angels and adopted a swan and an antelope, after which we have a succession of changes by various monarchs, among the supporters being two antelopes, a lion and an antelope, a lion and a white hart, a lion and a bull, two boars rampant and a red dragon (Wales) and a greyhound (Henry VII).

Henry VIII had dexter a lion rampant guardant crowned Or and sinister a dragon Gules. Edward VI for a wonder had the same, but Mary on her marriage to Philip of Spain impaled the arms of Spain and England and the dexter supporter became

113. *The Commonwealth*   114. *The Royal Arms,*
                            1707–14

an imperial eagle.

Queen Elizabeth I returned the lion rampant
guardant crowned Or to his position as dexter
supporter, and as sinister had the red dragon. On
the union with Scotland the supporters became a
lion and a unicorn, and there the supporters have
finally come to rest, in England at any rate.

The story of the Scottish arms is less complicated.
The lion rampant within a double tressure flory
counter-flory has been the Scottish coat since the
time of Alexander II and probably even earlier,
as the arms are believed to have been used by
William the Lion. The earliest *known* use of the
arms is in 1222. They have remained the same almost
continuously. For some peculiar reason, in 1471
the Scottish parliament decided to do away with
the tressure, but the Act never acquired force.

In 1558 it was enacted that the arms of the Dauphin of France be impaled with those of his wife Mary Queen of Scots but this was of short duration. During the Commonwealth, of course, Royal Arms were not used at all (Fig. 113), but the restoration soon put that right. It was bad heraldry on the part of Cromwell for the arms were of sovereignty and their continued use was quite reasonable. But no doubt he wanted as few reminders of the monarchy as possible.

When Scotland and England united, firstly in 1603 under one monarch and again in 1707 under one Parliament, the Scots displayed that independence which hallmarks them. It was all very well for England to give priority to the English arms, but it would not do in Scotland—and anyway it was the King of the Scots who had inherited England and not vice versa. And so it became the practice in Scotland to display the Scottish arms in the 1st and 4th quarters, and also to use the crest and supporters of Scotland. The Scottish crest is a lion sejeant Gules armed and langued Azure holding in the dexter paw a sword and in the sinister paw a sceptre, both proper. The supporters are both unicorns, crowned. The dexter one carries a banner charged with the Royal Arms of Scotland, and the sinister a banner Azure a saltire Argent. In 1672 Charles II registered two coats of arms in Scotland, first the quartered Royal arms and then the arms of the King of Scots, which was perfectly correct as he was King of Scotland as well as King of Great Britain.

115. *The Royal Arms,*
1801–16

116. *The Royal Arms,*
1816–37

This insistence on a proper regard for Scottish interests, within the Kingdom of Scotland, has through the centuries acquired official recognition by various Orders in Council, and there is now an official version of the Royal Arms for use in Scotland by all Scottish government departments and also on the Great Seal of Scotland. When used in Scotland the Royal Arms are encircled with the collar of the Thistle instead of the Garter. Each version of the Royal Arms may fairly be said to do justice to its own sovereign country while admitting the partnership of the other.

The Union Jack, which is the national flag of the United Kingdom, has gone through a few changes since its origin. Originally, in 1606, it was composed of the St Andrew's Cross with the St George's cross imposed on it, the latter being infimbriated white. In Scotland, needless to say, this was not popular, and St Andrew was imposed on St George. In 1801 St Patrick's cross was added, conjoined to the St Andrew's cross, and so the flag has remained, being a clever combination of three national flags.

CHAPTER XIII

THE POINT OF IT ALL

WE have now reached the stage where we are entitled to ask what is the point of it all. If it serves any purpose, we want to know what it is. What use is a grant of arms? Why should anybody apply for them? And quite often socialist peers *don't* apply for them.

If there is one thing which a grant of arms is not, it is not snobbish. The reason for this is that arms tell exactly and precisely what the owner is and indicate his precise position in society—whether he be gentleman or Duke. Snobbery, however one may care to define it, is fundamentally concerned with pretensions. There is nothing wrong, therefore, in applying for arms, or for displaying them in a normal way after they have been granted. Nobody who does so is giving himself airs—that is the one thing he is *not* doing.

Arms constitute a recognition by the Crown of the individual, and call for a record of that individual in public registers and official pedigrees. In the future, however obscure one's ancestral past might be and however difficult to trace the family tree, generations to come will have no trouble at all in going back at least to the grant of arms. So from that point of view they may prove useful at some unspecified future date.

Arms have a value as property, particularly to public corporations, commercial firms and so on who use them for purposes of advertising—what person in England who has looked at a daily newspaper has not seen, say, the arms of the Westminster Bank? Or Barclays?

A fact not always known is that a man may adopt as many different names as he pleases, and they will all be legal. A son need not even take his father's surname—there is no necessity to do so. But regardless of change of name, a man will only be granted one coat of arms. Furthermore, signatures are now necessary on legal documents, but it does no harm to sign *and* seal a document, and it is much easier to forge someone's signature than it is to forge it and also copy his engraved seal.

There is, I believe, inherent in practically all men a strong and lively sense of individual identity —nothing can satisfy it more than a coat of arms. Many thousands of men must sign themselves John Brown, but only one will have a particular coat of arms. *Azure a bend Or* is still as indicative of its owner today as it was in Chaucer's time. If there are any collateral Scropes we may be sure that their arms are different to some extent.

Finally there is the question of family honour. Why not have something tangible, some outward and visible sign that serves as an incentive to the family? A grant of arms, will not make a man noble in his character, but it will be a strong influence on his behaviour.

What can one do with arms after they have been granted, we may ask. Strangely enough heraldry has retained many of its original uses. Apart from signet rings and seals, which are very useful items for the armiger, most families have pieces of silverwear. What better way of marking knives and forks, the best silver spoons, silver ashtrays and salvers and so on than with the shield or the whole achievement. In the course of three or four generations quite a collection of silver may be acquired and it is less likely to be stolen and more likely to be the family's pride, if each piece is engraved with heraldry, rather than an ambiguous monogram. Think how many people have the initials A.B. and how few the arms *Per Pale Or and Gules, a chevron counterchanged.*

One of the most interesting uses of arms is for bookplates, which should always display the whole achievement. If they are simple black and white designs made from a line block, they cost very little indeed. Bookplates pasted inside the covers of one's more important books serve a useful and a decorative purpose. They help to render the books safe from that social pest, the person who borrows books and does not return them—it is liable to be embarrassing if all the books on one's bookshelves have the bookplates of one's friends. And, of course, the book is improved by this addition.

The use of bookplates is very old, and most of

*117. Balliol College,
Oxford*

the medieval books were decorated with heraldry.
Many thirteenth-, fourteenth- and fifteenth-century
psalters and missals with arms on their covers are
still in existence, and medieval wills books were often
identified by the arms on them. In 1399 Eleanor
Duchess of Gloucester bequeathed several volumes which were identified in this way.

All the foregoing has dealt with the acquisition
of personal arms. Heraldry, however, is not only of
interest to those who have arms of their own—
indeed many a person who is armigerous has no
interest whatever in heraldry outside his own
shield. Heraldry is one of the most fascinating and
rewarding of hobbies, especially for any person who
wants something that is not only absorbing but
unusual. It has the added advantage of being inexpensive.

There are very few rules in heraldry—most of
them which are necessary to a good start are already in this book—and one of the great things

about it is that one can either go into it deeply or treat it casually, yet at the same time the amount of pleasure derived from it remains constant.

One should study heraldry from its results rather than from books of rules, and once the simple rules have been mastered, nothing is more interesting than a few hours with a Burke's Landed Gentry or a Peerage. There is heraldry all around us in Britain, and how much of it has a story to tell, and what a story too, if only we were familiar with some of the arms we see displayed.

One of the more interesting aspects of life in Great Britain is its social uncertainty. The boy who today is not interested in fame and fortune may be the man who, tomorrow, has both thrust upon him. If, therefore, having got this far you simply are not interested, don't throw the book away. Put it at the back of the bookcase somewhere. You never know—

In twenty years' time you might *need* it!

118. *The present heraldic Crown*

INDEX

Figures in italics indicate the line drawings throughout the text.

147

148

149

Paris

- A  in the text denotes a highly recommended sight
- A complete A–Z of practical information starts on p. 104
- Extensive mapping throughout: on cover flaps and in text

Berlitz Publishing Company, Inc.

Princeton   Mexico City   Dublin   Eschborn   Singapore

Text: Martin Gostelow
Editors: Renée Ferguson, Peter Duncan
Photography: Pete Bennett
Layout: Media Content Marketing, Inc.
Cartography: Visual Image

Thanks to Giles Allen, Jack Altman; Eurostar for their assistance in the preparation of this guide.

Found an error we should know about? Our editor would be happy to hear from you, and a postcard would do. Although we make every effort to ensure the accuracy of all the information in this book, changes do occur.

ISBN 2-8315-6315-1
Revised 1998 – First Printing January 1998

Printed in Switzerland by Weber SA, Bienne
019/801 REV

CONTENTS

PARIS

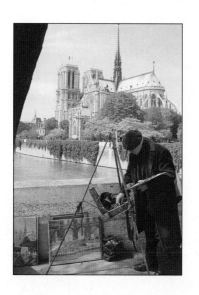

PARIS AND THE PARISIANS

It's no surprise that visitors flock to Paris. What other city can rival its combination of qualities? Magnificent monuments resonate with the echoes of a turbulent past. World-famous museums display unique treasures, in settings to match. All the amenities of a great capital are concentrated in a city on a human scale.

Throughout the ages Paris has always sent out seductive signals to the rest of the world: political freedom, sexual licence, revolutions in the arts, wonderful food, shops brimming with the good things of life. There were times not so long ago when the truth didn't match the myth. But not now. The art collections are as stunning, the shopping as enticing, the night life as varied as you could wish for.

Opera and ballet are both world class — the one staged in the modern Opéra-Bastille, the other in the finely restored 19th-century opera house, the Opéra Garnier. The jazz scene is vibrant, and other music from Algerian to Congolese finds the city a better showcase than its own homeland. Cinema is still accorded the status of an art — not only are the latest international releases shown, but laws also require a high percentage of home-grown productions to be screened on television and in the cinemas, keeping the local film industry busy.

A melting pot of people and cultures, France's capital has, surprisingly enough, no cuisine it can call its own — which doesn't matter because it can offer the pick of the regional dishes. Interpreted by today's creative chefs, French cuisine is lighter, brighter, fresher, and tastier than ever. And if you want a change you'll find plenty of alternatives among the wide range of ethnic and foreign restaurants.

> About 20% of the entire population of France lives in the greater Paris area.

Take a cruise on the Seine at sunset.

Take a seat at a café terrace and watch the world go by, at its pace or yours. The coffee or beer costs more than at the counter, but there's lots to see. Every passer-by seems to be giving a performance. Style is everything to Parisians, confident that they and their city are the centre of the universe and the focus of general admiration, not to say envy. A sometimes aloof exterior conceals a sensitive soul, caustic for sure, but alert and ready to engage in the battle of wits. To call someone an intellectual in France is still a compliment; philosophy, art, and social issues provide the mainstay of many a café conversation.

Just who is "the Parisian?" Among a Parisian population of over two million, only one in two is actually born in the capital. Most hail from the provinces, from Brittany, Burgundy, or Corsica — adding different ingredients to the Paris "stew" — and within a few years they are Parisian through and through, showing disdain for provincials (who return the compliment), while remaining fiercely loyal to the province they left. Successive waves of refugees have also found a home here and left their marks: Jews, Armenians, Russians after 1917 (not all of them aristocrats), and Spanish Republicans during their Civil War. More recently have come large immigrant populations from north and west Africa and French territories in the Caribbean. Noone denies that there are problems of assimilation. It can only be hoped that time will gradually allay them.

Paris has not only restored buildings and built new structures, but it has also altered its image over the past two decades. It is now a clean city. Battalions of green-clad men and women and fleets of futuristic machines see to that. And yes, the plumbing works. You can go for days without meeting one of the famously surly waiters, shop assistants, or taxi drivers of the past. There's scarcely a hotel that hasn't been recently renovated, a public building that hasn't been scrubbed. Fresh paint and new gilding shines wherever you look. Of course, there is another side to the coin: the usual big city afflictions of high unemployment, beggars in the métro, and people without a home living in cardboard boxes.

Street perfcormers at Les Halles — formerly a food market, now a garden.

A sense of style is a Paris hallmark.

When former President Mitterrand launched a programme of dramatic new building projects in 1981, he took the view that the state had an important role to play in the development of the capital. In doing so he was continuing in the tradition of several earlier French leaders. François I, Henri IV, Louis XIV, and Napoleon all contributed to Paris's harmonious blend of styles. Napoleon III's planner Baron Haussmann cut ruthlessly through the old medieval maze of streets to give the city the wide avenues and boulevards that define its appearance to this day. Strict architectural codes allowed Paris to miss out on the fad for high-rises. Only the Montparnasse skyscraper disturbs the near skyline: the towers and Grande Arche of La Défense on the distant horizon are only mildly obtrusive. The Pompidou Centre, Forum des Halles, and Opéra-Bastille all caused bitter controversy, but in different ways brought new dynamism to a faded environment.

Each of the 20 *arrondissements*, or districts (see page 26), has its own character. Ethnic groups lend an exotic air to one street, while the next harbours the discreet apartments of the ultra-rich. A stately avenue spawns a tangle of little streets. Former working-class areas have become the height of chic, upstaging some formerly chic areas which have slid into decline.

Villages that were absorbed as Paris developed have retained their individuality, their little shops and country-style markets.

The Left Bank remains distinct from the Right. Publishing houses and many art galleries and bookshops lie on the Left, the *rive gauche*, the intellectuals' bank, while the Right Bank has always attracted the Establishment: big names in fashion and cuisine, banks, offices, and grand hotels. But it isn't that simple. Since in general French hearts lie on the Left and their wallets on the Right, many have a foot in both camps. So galleries and fashion houses often have branches on both banks. Before and after World War II the young made a beeline for the Left Bank, leaving the Right to the rich and the "Philistines," but now evenings can be far livelier around the transformed Les Halles, Beaubourg, and Bastille than in the boulevards or lanes of Saint-Germain and Montparnasse.

Ça va? –
How's it going?

Ça va bien. –
Doin' fine.

When to visit Paris depends on your own preference and time. Each season has its distinct charms. A Parisian winter is nothing to dread; indeed, the classical façades seem to look their best under a cold, crisp light. Golden autumn holds as much romance as spring, when just a hint of sunshine brings café tables spilling out onto the terraces and the gardens come to life. In the heat of August half of Paris takes off on holiday and many restaurants close. Whenever you choose to go you can watch life, window shop, or just wander — there's always something happening.

Patriotism on display in a Paris window.

A BRIEF HISTORY

Origins

Defence came first, beauty simply followed. A Celtic tribe called the Parisii settled on an island in the River Seine, the present Ile de la Cité, around 300 B.C. Lutetia (marshland), as it was known, developed into a prosperous town, even issuing its own gold coins. The river, far wider than now, protected it against most invaders, but not the Romans, who took it in 52 B.C. during Julius Caesar's conquest of Gaul.

The Right Bank of the river was too marshy to live on, so the town expanded to the Left Bank, in the area of the present Latin Quarter. In their customary fashion, the Romans built temples, straight roads, markets, and bridges. The massive remains of their public baths still stand, right opposite the Sorbonne (see page 55). St. Denis brought Christianity to the city and was rewarded by decapitation on the hill of Montmartre in around 250 A.D.

Towards the close of the third century, much of Roman Gaul was overrun by Germanic tribes of Huns and Franks, but Lutetia shrank back to the fortified Ile de la Cité and held out. In 486, by now known as Paris, the city fell to Clovis, king of the Franks. He became a convert to Christianity, and several religious foundations date from this time. The Left Bank was occupied once again and the church of Saint-Germain-des-Prés was built there in the sixth century.

A Capital Is Born

From 861, the Vikings plundered Paris at regular intervals. It remained a backwater on the European scene until Hugues Capet, Count of Paris, was elected King of France in 987. Under the Capetian dynasty, Paris grew to be the economic

Historical Landmarks

ca 300 B.C. Celtic settlement on island in the River Seine

52 B.C. Roman conquest, followed by expansion to Left Bank

486 Paris falls to Franks led by Clovis

987 Hugues Capet elected King of France

ca. 1200 Building of Notre-Dame cathedral begins

1420 English occupy Paris

1431 Henry VI of England crowned King of France

1436 English expelled

1594 Henri IV enters Paris

1682 Louis XIV moves court to Versailles

1789 French Revolution

1793 Execution of Louis XVI and Marie Antoinette; Reign of Terror

1804 Napoleon becomes emperor

1814 Fall of Napoleon; restoration of Bourbon monarchy

1815 Brief return of Napoleon (known as The 100 Days)

1830 "Bourgeois revolution"; Louis-Philippe, the Citizen King

1848 Revolution brings Louis-Napoleon to power

1870 Franco-Prussian War; Second Empire ends; Paris besieged

1871 Paris Commune — brief period of workers' rule

1900 First Métro line opened

1914–18 World War I

1939–45 World War II

1940 French government capitulates; Germans occupy Paris

1944 Free French and other Allied forces liberate Paris

1958 Fall of Fourth Republic; De Gaulle becomes president

1968 Student riots and demonstrations

1973 Périphérique ring road completed, running around Paris

1977 Jacques Chirac becomes first elected mayor since 1871

1995 Jacques Chirac elected president

and political capital. Its merchants exploited the commerce of the Seine and brought prosperity to the city; the importance of the river to early Paris is reflected in the old motto, *Fluctuat nec mergitur* (It has its ups and downs but doesn't sink), and the ship on its flag. The port area, known as the Grève, developed on the Right Bank by the present-day Châtelet and Hôtel de Ville. (To this day, the French for "on strike" is *en grève*, because striking workers would congregate in the area.)

Revenues from river trade financed the lengthy building of Notre-Dame, and enabled Philippe Auguste (1180–1223) to construct a fortress named the Louvre, as well as various aqueducts, fresh-water fountains, and paved streets. To protect his investment while away on the Third Crusade (1189–1192), he surrounded the city with walls.

The Roman baths at Musée National du Moyen Age are a sign of the city's early past.

Louis IX, a.k.a. Saint Louis (1226–1270, canonized 1297) patronized the spiritual and intellectual side of Paris, building the Gothic masterpiece, the church of Sainte-Chapelle and many colleges on the Left Bank. In time the colleges evolved into a university which took its name from one of them, La Sorbonne, established by the chaplain to the king, Robert de Sorbon. By the end of Louis's reign, Paris had become one of the greatest cities in Western Christendom, with a population of 100,000.

In the 14th century, plague (or the "Black Death") and the Hundred Years' War with England drained France. In 1356, with King Jean le Bon held prisoner at Poitiers, the leader of the Paris merchants, Etienne Marcel, took advantage of the resulting confusion and set up a municipal dictatorship. Though assassinated two years later, Marcel had shown that the Parisians were a force to be reckoned with. Wary of their militancy, the subsequent king, Charles V, constructed the Bastille fortress.

If the 14th century had been unsettling for Paris, the 15th century opened even more disastrously. In 1407, the Duke of Burgundy had the Duke of Orleans murdered on the rue Barbette, leading to 12 years of strife between their supporters. The Burgundians called in the help of the English, who entered Paris in 1420. Ten years later, Joan of Arc tried and failed to liberate the city, and in the following year came worse humiliation: the young English King Henry VI was crowned King of France in Notre-Dame cathedral. However, the English triumph was short-lived: they were soon expelled from the city, and by 1453 had lost all their French possessions but Calais.

Royal Patrons

With François I (1515–1547), the city learned to thrive under an absolutist and absent monarch, busy with wars in Italy and even a year's imprisonment in Spain. The arts, sciences, and literature flourished. Much of the Louvre was torn down and rebuilt along the present lines. A new Hôtel de Ville (town hall) was begun, as well as the superb Saint-Eustache church. Parisians were already assuming their distinctive pride in the uniqueness of their city. The poet Villon sang: *Il n'y a bon bec que de Paris* (Only Parisians have real wit), while Pierre de Ronsard recorded a view of Paris as "the city imbued with the discipline and glory of the muses."

Bloody religious wars later wreaked havoc and mayhem, starting in 1572 with the infamous St. Bartholomew's Day massacre of 3,000 Protestants in Paris and culminating in the siege of the city by Henri de Navarre in 1589. Before the Catholic League capitulated, 13,000 Parisians had died of starvation. Henri was crowned at Chartres and finally entered the capital in 1594 — but not before he had turned Catholic himself, noting famously (and ambiguously) that "Paris is well worth a mass."

Henri IV did Paris proud once he was its master. He built the beautiful place des Vosges and place Dauphine, embellished the banks of the river with the quais de l'Arsenal, de l'Horloge, and des Orfèvres, and even constructed the Samaritaine hydraulic machine that pumped fresh water to Right Bank households up until 1813. Most popular of France's monarchs, *le bon roi Henri* (good King Henry) was also a notorious ladies' man. He completed the Pont-Neuf (the oldest bridge in Paris) as well as the adjacent gardens, where he was known to dally with his ladies.

During the reign of Louis XIII (1610–1643), Paris began to take on the fashionable aspect that became its hallmark. Elegant houses sprang up along the rue du Faubourg-Saint-Honoré, and the magnificent *hôtels* (mansions) of the nobility mushroomed in the Marais. The capital consolidated its growing position as the hub of the country with the establishment of a royal printing press, the Académie Française of Cardinal Richelieu, and in gaining ecclesiastical status as an archbishopric.

Paris increasingly attracted nobles from the provinces — too many for the liking of Louis XIV, *le roi Soleil* (the Sun King — 1643–1715). To bring his overly powerful and independent aristocrats back into line, Louis decided to move the

The early 17th-century place des Vosges remains one of the most beautiful squares in Paris.

court out of the capital to Versailles, compelling them to live at vast expense in his enormous new palace. Paris lost most of its political clout, but looked more impressive than ever with the landscaping of the Tuileries Gardens and the Champs-Elysées, the building of the Louvre's great colonnade and the Invalides hospital for wounded and retired soldiers. The city continued to assert its cultural ascendancy with the organization of the new academies of the arts, literature, and sciences and the establishment of the Comédie-Française (1680) and several other theatres. The population increased to 560,000, almost six times as many as in the 13th century.

The Sun King's successors, the indolent Louis XV (1715–1774) and the inept Louis XVI, became increasingly unpopular, even hated, as corruption ruled and their ministers tried to raise taxes to pay for costly foreign wars. One of the final construction projects of the *ancien Régime* (the old, or pre-revolutionary regime) was a new 23km (14-mile) wall running around the perimeter of the city. Begun in 1784, this became a major factor in the coming unrest, for it was along the wall that taxes were collected on the various goods brought into the city.

Revolution

The 1789 French Revolution was not the first to break out in Paris, nor the last, nor even the bloodiest, but its effects were the most far-reaching. Starting with protests by the gentry about taxes, it was taken up by the middle classes (the *bourgeoisie*), who wanted to cut the privileges of the monarchy,

The story of the Revolution that turned the world upside down is told at the Musée Carnavalet.

aristocracy, and church. And it was middle-class intellectuals who then stirred up the urban poor, the previously powerless *sans-culottes* (people without breeches) to revolt.

A climax was reached on 21 January 1793, with the public beheading of Louis XVI in the place de la Révolution, nowadays called place de la Concorde. In the Reign of Terror later that year (Year I of the new calendar), many perceived enemies of the new republic followed Louis to the guillotine. Several were revolutionaries themselves: Desmoulins, the fiery orator, and Danton, who tried to moderate the Terror, and then the men who had organized it, Robespierre and Saint-Just.

In 1799, Napoleon Bonaparte imposed his authority as effective dictator, and later as emperor. Frequent absences on foreign business did not hinder his projects for making Paris the capital of Europe. Detailed maps of the city and architectural plans for new buildings never left his side. Visitors can see Napoleon's mark in spectacular monuments, such as the Arc de Triomphe and the column of the Grande-Armée on the Place Vendôme, but the Emperor himself was proudest of his civic improvements: fresh water in quantity throughout the city, improved drainage, new food markets, a streamlined municipal administration and police force. The majority of his reforms survived his fall in 1814 and final defeat the following year, and became a model for modern urban government.

The monarchy returned, but the concentration in Paris of an ambitious bourgeoisie, dissatisfied workers, and radical intellectuals was an ever-present threat. In July 1830, protest turned to riots and the building of barricades. Charles X, who in the Bourbon tradition had "forgotten nothing and learned nothing" from history, was forced to abdicate. But instead of restoring the republic, the revolutionary leaders played safe and agreed to the accession of the moderate Louis-Philippe, the "Citizen King."

The Revolution of 1848, which brought Louis-Philippe's "bourgeois" monarchy to an end, likewise started with riots and barricades in the streets of Paris. A mob threatened the royal palace, forcing him to flee, and then invaded the Chamber of Deputies demanding a republic. Elections followed, but they showed that however radical Paris might be, the rest of France was still largely conservative. The new National Assembly withdrew the concessions that had been made to the workers; and up went the barricades again. This time the army was called in with its heavy guns. At least 1,500 insurrectionists were killed, and thousands deported.

A new democratic system was adopted and might have worked, but in voting for a president the people voted for a name, Louis-Napoleon, the nephew of the dead emperor. In 1851 he seized absolute power, and the next year became Emperor Napoleon III. (The second of the line, son of the first, never reigned and died young.)

Capital Facelift

It was fear that led Napoleon III to modernize Paris. The insurrections of 1830 and 1848 had flared up in the densely populated working-class districts around the centre, and he wanted to prevent any chance of a recurrence. He therefore commissioned Baron Georges Haussmann to do away with the clusters of narrow streets and alleys that nurtured discontent. The baron razed them and moved the occupants out to the suburbs, creating the "red belt" which makes Paris one of the few Western capitals whose suburbs are not predominantly conservative. This ruthless approach made way for a new Paris, far removed from the old in looks and spirit, but with its own charm. Broad boulevards and avenues highlighted the monuments, churches, and public buildings. As the baron explained to his emperor, these avenues were too wide for barricades and gave the artillery a clear line of fire in case of revolt.

This Second Empire was also a time of joyous abandon and boisterous expansion, depicted in Offenbach's operettas. But the emperor stumbled. After a foolish declaration of war against Prussia in 1870, the army of Napoleon III was quickly defeated. His disgrace and capture brought the proclamation of a new republic, followed by a crippling siege of Paris by the Prussians. The city held out, though reduced to starvation level, and communicated with the rest of the country by means of balloons (bearing pigeons to bring messages back). When France's leaders agreed to peace, there was yet another uprising. The Paris Commune (self-rule by the workers) lasted 10 weeks, from 18 March to 29 May 1871, until Adolphe Thiers, first president of the Third Republic, sent in troops from Versailles to crush it. The *communards* were pushed back street by street and in the last days set fire to the Tuileries palace and other buildingss, and executed hostages, including the Archbishop of Paris. The government took its vengeance: at least 20,000 Commune supporters were killed in the fighting or executed afterwards.

Ups and Downs

In spite of the horrors of siege and civil war, prosperity rapidly returned and the capital's resurrection was marked by a great construction boom. Projects begun under Napoleon III, such as the opera house and the huge Les Halles market, were completed. Star of the show was the Eiffel Tower (built in 1889), as techniques using iron improved. By the end of the 19th century, the splendid new *métro* began to provide fast and comfortable transport across the city.

Artists, writers, and revolutionaries flocked to this hub of creative activity. Picasso came over from Barcelona in 1900, followed by Modigliani from Livorno, Soutine from Minsk, Stravinsky from St. Petersburg, and Gertrude Stein from San Francisco. Then ensued a long stream of American artists and writers led by Ernest Hemingway and F. Scott Fitzgerald.

Two wars, of course, took their toll. The Germans threatened but failed to take Paris during World War I, but they occupied it for four long and unhappy years (1940–1944) during World War II. Liberation came eventually, with a parade by General de Gaulle and his Free French forces down the Champs-Elysées. Unlike many great European capitals, Paris escaped large-scale bombing and Hitler's vengeful order to burn the city before retreating had mercifully been ignored. After World War II, recovery was slow as governments came and went in rapid succession. The Fourth Republic died, unregretted, in 1958, following an army revolt at the time of the colonial war in Algeria. Recalled from retirement, General de Gaulle thus became the first president of the Fifth Republic and set about restoring French prestige and morale.

ICI EST TOMBÉ
POUR LA LIBÉRATION DE PARIS
LE 22 AOÛT 1944
ROGER LAMBERT
AGÉ DE 19 ANS

Some who fought against the occupation did not live to see the Liberation. The others remember.

Recent Times

In May 1968 Parisian students and workers recaptured some of the old revolutionary spirit. Walls were daubed

with slogans and the Latin Quarter's paving stones were hurled at the smugly entrenched Establishment. But national elections showed that, as so often in the past, Paris was at odds with most of France, which voted for stability. Succeeding de Gaulle, Georges Pompidou picked up the pieces and affirmed the new prosperity with riverside expressways and skyscrapers, and the controversial Beaubourg cultural centre which bears his name.

In 1977 Jacques Chirac became the first democratically elected mayor of Paris. (For more than a century, since the stormy days of the Commune, the national government controlled the city through its own appointed officials.) In a country where politicians are allowed to double as mayor and prime minister, Parisians benefit from leaders keen to further their national political ambitions with a dynamic municipal performance. Chirac made the most of his opportunity, and is credited with, among other accomplishments, the effective clean-up of the formerly dirty streets.

Former President François Mitterrand made his own mark on the Paris skyline with a series of innovative and impressive works: the Grande Arche, the Opéra-Bastille, the Institut du Monde Arabe, and the reorganization of the Louvre around a great glass pyramid. Some of these projects were timed for completion in 1989, when the 200th anniversary of the Revolution was celebrated in style.

Jacques Chirac at last relinquished the mayor's job when he was elected president in 1995, the culmination of a persistent 20-year campaign. Poised on the eve of the 21st century, Paris has probably never looked better. Monuments shine with fresh layers of gold leaf, new and remodelled museums display its heritage, and the city continues to wield an astonishing cultural influence throughout the world.

WHERE TO GO

GETTING AROUND

As soon as you can, buy a Museum Pass (see page 74) to save money and avoid waiting at ticket desks, and a carnet, a book of 10 métro tickets (good for buses too) or, better still, one of the special passes which give even greater savings (see page 123).

To get your bearings, picture Paris as a circle, with the river Seine threading across the centre, flanked by famous landmarks — Notre-Dame, the Louvre, place de la Concorde, the Eiffel Tower. Bridges of all shapes and sizes tie the Right (north) and Left Banks together or link them to the two islands in the middle, Ile de la Cité and Ile Saint-Louis.

This is one of the easiest of large cities to get about. The modernized **métro** system is smooth, regular, and fast, with low, flat-rate fares. **RER** commuter trains can also take you rapidly to places on the outskirts. **Buses** give you a sightseeing tour at a bargain price, while adhering to schedules as far as traffic allows (rush hours can create terrible jams). **Taxis** provide a lazy alternative.

> Underground fare in Paris is the same irrespective of the distance you travel.

Bus tours take you to the big attractions, but inevitably at times when they are busiest. Some tour buses which take you round the highlights let you hop on and off, wherever and as often as you like, all on one ticket, for a period of up to 48 hours. Tourist information offices (see page 121) have details. **Bicycle** hire companies (see page 106) also run tours. If you want to sightsee in style (and expensively) you can even see Paris from a helicopter, plane, or hot-air balloon.

A **boat cruise** on the Seine is one of the best introductions to the city. While you glide along, multilingual commentaries tell you about the sights. Boats run from about 10:00 A.M. to 10:30 P.M. Most tour boats provide a choice of open-air and glassed-in seating, some offer lunch and dinner, and trips last 60 to 75 minutes. Canal tours reveal a less grand face of Paris on the way from the centre to Parc de la Villette (see page 72) in the northeastern suburbs. The trip takes three hours, with a tunnel and several locks to be negotiated.

Cruises on the Seine provide a good first look at the city. But for transportation, the métro is hard to beat.

Parisians themselves often use the *Bat-O-Bus* (river bus) for travelling east or west and avoiding traffic snarls. It runs from May to September; stops are at the Eiffel Tower, Musée d'Orsay, Louvre, Notre-Dame, and Hôtel de Ville. It's expensive, but you may prefer the absence of commentary.

Central Paris is surprisingly compact, and most hotels are close to many of the sights. So if time isn't a major factor, the best way of getting the feel of the place is to **walk**. All you need is a pair of comfortable shoes and a **map**. The big department stores and hotels give away millions of street maps each year. Métro stations display good maps of their local district as well as the métro itself, and give out pocket plans

Paris by Numbers

The city is divided into 20 districts or *arrondissements*, the numbers spiralling outwards like a snail's shell, starting at the centre around the Louvre. When Parisians refer to the 5th *(cinquième)*, or 16th *(seizième)*, for example, they have a clear image of the sorts of shop, restaurant, housing, and people to be found there.

Here's an idea of the way the districts divide:

1er: the Louvre to Les Halles, and half of Ile de la Cité

2e: south of the *grands boulevards*; financial district, many theatres

3e: quiet, old streets of the northern Marais

4e: Pompidou Centre to southern Marais; Jewish quarter

5e: Latin Quarter; educational institutions and student life

6e: Saint-Germain-des-Prés; intellectuals, bookshops, restaurants

7e: Musée d'Orsay to the Eiffel Tower; elegant apartments

8e: Champs-Elysées to Madeleine; luxury shops, fashion houses

9e: Opéra-Garnier and big department stores

10e: Gare du Nord; not many sights; walks along Canal St. Martin

11e: Bastille; trendy galleries, night-life, farther north, Oberdampf, the new "in" scene

12e: bordering on Bois de Vincennes; nearby zoo

13e: tower blocks; large Far Eastern community

14e: Montparnasse; commercial development, cafés

15e: rue de Vaugirard (Paris' longest street); food markets

16e: Arc de Triomphe to Bois de Boulogne; expensive apartments

17e: residential chic; food shops on rue Lévis

18e: Montmartre; village life and low life

19e and 20e: Père Lachaise, Belleville; poor suburbs and La Villette

Street numbering follows a rough pattern. The lower numbers are generally nearest the Seine, with evens on the right and odds on the left as you move away from the river. Streets parallel to the river are numbered in an upstream-downstream direction.

of the métro and bus routes. More and more streets and entire areas like Les Halles and Beaubourg have been pedestrianized, adding to the profusion of parks, squares, and gardens.

THE ISLANDS

Ile de la Cité

Fittingly for the cradle of a town that grew from its river commerce, the Ile de la Cité is shaped like a boat, with the green, shaded **square du Vert Galant** pointing downstream. From the first settlement built by the original Parisii until the middle of the 19th century, the pocket-sized island lay at the heart of the city. The heavy-handed Baron Haussmann (see page 20) then swept away virtually all the medieval and 17th-century structures, leaving just place Dauphine and rue Chanoinesse (the ancient home of the cathedral canons) as signs of the island's once rich residential life.

The baron was also toying with the idea of replacing the gracious red-brick houses of the triangular place Dauphine with a neo-Grecian colonnaded square when, thankfully, he was forced out of office for juggling the books. Near the lively **Pont-Neuf**, the *place* (square) was built in 1607 by Henri IV in honour of his son the *dauphin* (or future king, Louis XIII). Sadly, only numbers 14 and 26 are still in their original state.

The huge **Palais de Justice**, heart of the centralized French legal system, stands on the site of the Roman palace where the Emperor Julian was crowned in 360. Together with the Conciergerie (see pages 28–29), it sprawls right across the Ile de la Cité. Concealed in the courtyard between them is a Gothic masterpiece, the **Sainte-Chapelle**, whose fine proportions stand in sharp contrast to the ponderous palace. The chapel was constructed in 1248 to house holy relics, Christ's Crown of Thorns and a fragment of the True Cross, which the pious Louis IX (later canonized as Saint Louis) had bought from the Byzantine emperor. If you can, arrive as the chapel opens or at sunset (see page 37) and make your way to the upper level, where light blazes in through 15 stained-glass windows separated by buttresses so slim that there seems to be no wall at all. Miraculously, of the 1,134 individual pieces of glass, 720 are 13th-century originals. Concerts are held here regularly: such a setting could hardly be bettered.

Between 1789 and 1815 the chapel assumed various guises: a flour warehouse during the Revolution and a club for high-ranking dandies, then an archive for Napoleon's Consulate. It was this latter role that saved the chapel from projected destruction, since the bureaucrats could not think of another site in which to put their mountains of paper.

These days, bureaucrats find room for their papers in the Palais de Justice and the nearby **Préfecture de Police**, haunt of those fictional detectives, Inspectors Maigret and Clouseau. The great lobby of the Palais, the Salle des Pas Perdus, is worth a visit for a glimpse of the many lawyers, plaintiffs, witnesses, court reporters, and assorted hangers-on waiting nervously for the wheels of French justice to grind into action.

Their anxiety is nothing compared with that of the prisoners once held in the forbidding **Conciergerie**,

Once a prison, the Conciergerie now looks quietly over the Seine and Pont au Change.

reached from the quai de l'Horloge. Part of the 14th-century royal palace, it was probably named after the *Compte des Cierges* (Count of the Candles), who was traditionally in charge of punishments; slowly it took on the role of a prison. In 1793, at the height of the Terror, it was literally the "antechamber of the guillotine." Queen Marie-Antoinette, Robespierre, Danton, and Saint-Just all spent their last nights in

---

Bridges of Paris

Within the city, no fewer than 36 bridges span the Seine. Whether you are walking or riding, there are some that you'll use frequently, and they're a big feature of the river cruises.

Pont-Neuf (new bridge) is in fact the oldest survivor, dating from 1606, the reign of Henri IV — seen on horseback at the centre. It was kept free of the houses that lined earlier bridges, and soon became, and still is, a popular place to meet and stroll. Some of the hawkers, musicians, pickpockets, and tooth-pullers who used to gather here are caricatured in grimacing stone heads on the cornice facing the river.

Pont des Arts is the next downstream, a spidery iron structure also reserved for walkers and a favourite meeting point on the way to the Latin Quarter.

Pont-Royal crosses where the Louvre meets the Tuileries gardens and gives a great view of both, as well as the Musée d'Orsay on the other bank. It was built for Louis XIV in 1685.

Pont de la Concorde was started before the Revolution and completed in 1790, using stones from the dismantled Bastille. Its original name of Pont Louis XVI was duly changed to Pont de la Révolution the year before the king went to the guillotine nearby in place de la Révolution (now Concorde).

Pont Alexandre III was named after the Tsar of Russia whose successor, Nicholas II, laid the first stone in 1896. It was the first bridge with a single steel arch, and the widest. The cast-iron lamp standards are characteristic of its era, the Belle Epoque, and gilded statues at the ends depict medieval and modern France (Right Bank), and France of the Renaissance and Louis XIV (Left Bank).

the Galerie des Prisonniers. The Salle des Girondins displays a guillotine blade, the crucifix to which Marie-Antoinette prayed, and the lock used on Robespierre's cell. Look out on the Cour des Femmes, where husbands, lovers, wives, and mistresses were allowed one final tryst before the tumbrels came to carry off the condemned. About 2,500 victims of the Revolutionary guillotine spent their last hours in the Conciergerie.

Notre-Dame

Stonework in delicate lace patterns outlines the windows of Notre-Dame Cathedral.

The site of the cathedral of Notre-Dame de Paris has had a religious role for at least 2,000 years. In Roman times a temple to Jupiter stood here; some stone fragments unearthed in 1711 can be seen in the Musée du Moyen Age (see page 72). In the fourth century, the first Christian church, Saint-Etienne, was built, joined two centuries later by a second church, dedicated to Notre-Dame. Viking and Norman raids left both in a sorry state, and Bishop Maurice de Sully decided a cathedral should be built to replace them. Begun in 1163, the main part of Notre-Dame took no less than 167 years to finish, and thus spanned the transition from Romanesque to Gothic.

The cathedral has been the setting for numerous momentous occasions: in 1239 Louis IX walked barefoot through it with his holy treasure, the Crown of Thorns (before the Sainte-Chapelle was built); in 1430 it saw Henry VI of England crowned King of France (see page 15); in 1594 Henri IV attended the mass that sealed his conversion to Catholicism and reinforced his hold on the French throne. Here in 1804 Napoleon crowned himself as emperor, upstaging the Pope, who had come to Paris expecting to do it. More recently, the cathedral held the state funeral of de Gaulle.

Across the three doorways of the west front, the 28 statues of the **Galerie des Rois** represent the kings of Judah. These are 19th-century restorations: the originals were torn down during the Revolution because they were thought to depict kings of France (a number are preserved in the Musée du Moyen Age, see page 72). The superb central **rose window** depicts the Redemption after the Fall: the view of it from the inside is partly blocked by the huge organ. Two more outsized rose windows illuminate the transept; the northern window, incredibly, retains most of its 13th-century glass. Don't miss the 14th-centu-

The flower market at place Louis Lépine on Ile de La Cité switches to selling caged birds on Sunday.

ry **Virgin and Child** that bears the cathedral's name, Notre-Dame de Paris (Our Lady of Paris), to the right of the choir entrance.

The original architect of the Cathedral of Notre-Dame is unknown, but Pierre de Montreuil (who was involved in the building of Sainte-Chapelle) was responsible for a large part of the 13th-century work. The present state of the cathedral owes a great deal to Eugène Viollet-le-Duc, who laboured patiently from 1845 to 1863 to restore it following the ravages of the 18th century, caused by pre-Revolutionary meddlers as well as the Revolutionaries who stripped it of

It sometimes seems as if time has stood still in the quiet streets of Ile Saint-Louis.

its religious symbols and declared it a "Temple of Reason."

The long climb up the **north tower** may be strenuous (there are 245 steps), but the wonderful views of Paris and close-ups of the roof and gargoyles make it well worth the effort. Once up there, you can cross to the south tower to see the 13-ton bell, the only one remaining — the Revolutionaries melted down all the others to make cannon. The bell was re-cast in the 1680s. A further 124 steps lead to the top of the south tower for still more spectacular views.

Baron Haussmann greatly enlarged the *parvis*, or square, in front of the cathedral, diminishing the impact of its towering west front. The **crypt** beneath the square contains walls and foundations from the Gallic, Roman, and medieval eras, and a brilliantly designed exhibition on early Paris.

Ile Saint-Louis

Though connected by a bridge, the sister islands are far apart in spirit. The Ile Saint-Louis, formed by joining and draining two mudbanks in the 17th century, is a sanctuary of gracious living, its quiet streets lined by elegant houses and mansions, where rich artists, politicians, doctors, actresses, and heiresses have lived. President Pompidou had a house on the quai de Béthune and used to escape there from the Elysée Palace as frequently as he could.

The most striking of the mansions, the **Hôtel Lauzun**, at 17 quai d'Anjou, was built in the 1650s by Le Vau, who also worked on the Seine façade of the Louvre and the Versailles château. The **Hôtel Lambert**, another very impressive mansion designed by Le Vau for the Sun King's secretary, stands on the corner of the rue Saint-Louis-en-l'Ile. Voltaire once enjoyed a tempestuous love affair here with the lady of the house, the marquise du Châtelet. The church of **Saint-Louis-en-l'Ile** is airy and bright, and a golden light illuminates a good collection of Dutch, Flemish, and Italian 16th- and 17th-century art.

From the western end of the shady quai d'Orléans, you'll have a splendid view of the apse of Notre-Dame, although the majority of pilgrims to this spot are more intent on a visit to Berthillon, the celebrated maker of ice creams and delicious sorbets.

RIGHT BANK

From ultra-chic to downright sleazy, the Right Bank (*rive droite*) covers the most fashionable shopping areas, the presidential Elysée Palace, the *grands boulevards* and financial district, and, farther north, seamy Clichy and Pigalle, as well as hilly Montmartre, where modern art could be said to have begun. Back in the middle of it all, the enormous Louvre museum stands as a magnificent challenge, and just to the east of the central area, Les Halles, Beaubourg (around the Pompidou Centre), and place de la Bastille have each been transformed by controversial projects: the variety and energy of their nightlife has overtaken that of the Left Bank. Half forgotten and thereby saved from such schemes, the charming old Marais and Jewish quarter preserve the old Paris of the 17th century.

☞ Place Charles-de-Gaulle (l'Etoile)

Known as the place de l'Etoile until the death of Charles de Gaulle in 1969, this great circular space with its whirling

There's a fine view from the Arc de Triomphe.

traffic is dominated by the vast **Arc de Triomphe** (50 metres high and 45 metres wide, or 164 feet by 148 feet). A trip to the top by elevator, or around 300 steps, affords spectacular views. The star (*l'Etoile*) is formed by 12 avenues radiating outwards in a tour de force of geometric planning which cannot really be taken in at ground level.

The Arc de Triomphe was conceived by Napoleon I as a tribute to his armies, and bears the names of hundreds of his marshals and generals, and dozens of victories. No defeats are recorded, naturally, although a few of the victories are debatable. Napoleon himself only ever saw a wood and canvas model: the arch was completed during the 1830s. It soon became the focus for state occasions, such as the return of the ex-emperor's own remains from St. Helena in 1840 and the funeral of Victor Hugo in 1885. In 1920, the Unknown Soldier of World War I was buried at the arch; three years later the eternal flame was lit. When Adolf Hitler arrived in Paris as a conqueror in 1940, the Arc de Triomphe was the first place he wanted to see. And at the Liberation this was the spot where General de Gaulle commenced his triumphal march down the Champs-Elysées.

Guard at the Elysée Palace.

Avenue Foch, leading away from l'Etoile to the Bois de Boulogne, is one of the most majestic of the city's residential avenues. It is one of the most exclusive, too, though somewhat democratized these days by the groups of *boules* players on its gravelled side paths. Avenue de la Grande-Armée points straight to Neuilly and the towers of La Défense with the Grande Arche behind.

Avenue des Champs-Elysées

It's fashionable nowadays to look down on the Champs-Elysées (Parisians may inform you they never set foot there), but despite extensive commercialization it remains one of the finest avenues anywhere in the world, straight as a rod, sloping at a gentle pace down to the place de la Concorde and fringed by chestnut trees, the object of careful replanting to ensure that it retains its elegant beauty.

The top two-thirds of the avenue are filled with cinemas, airline offices and car showrooms, the excellent **tourist information office** (number 127), and café terraces that make perfect, if slightly expensive, vantage points for people-watching.

Below the Rond-Point, the mood changes and a pleasant park leads you past two landmarks: the **Petit Palais**, all steel and glass, and the **Grand Palais**. Both were constructed for the Universal Exhibition of 1900 and are today used for a variety of exhibitions, though the Petit Palais houses several permanent collections of 19th-century French paintings. The Grand Palais shares its colossal building with the Palais de la Découverte (see page 75), and includes among its displays a hands-on exhibition of the sciences, with a planetarium as centre-piece.

The expansive **place de la Concorde** was designed by Jacques-Ange Gabriel as place Louis XV in 1753, but the Revolution dispensed with all royal connotations. The king's statue was replaced by a guillotine, soon to be used to behead Louis XVI and more than 1,000 other victims. In 1934 it was the scene of bloody rioting against the government;

Paris Highlights

Arc de Triomphe. Honours Napoleon's armies and their victories. The view from the top is superb. Open 9:30A.M. – 11P.M., Tuesday – Saturday, to 6:30P.M. Sunday, Monday (winter 10A.M. – 5P.M. daily). Métro: Charles de Gaulle-Etoile.

Eiffel Tower. The world's tallest structure when it was built in 1889, and still a marvel. Open daily 9:30A.M. – 11P.M. (July and August 9A.M. – midnight). Métro: Bir-Hakeim, Ecole Militaire, Trocadéro.

La Défense. The Grande Arche is the high point (literally and figuratively) of this development. Open always. Grande Arche roof: open 9A.M. – 7P.M. (8P.M. Saturday, Sunday, holidays). Closes one hour earlier, October – March. Métro: Grande Arche de la Défense.

Les Halles. Formerly a food market, now a garden. The glitzy Forum des Halles shopping complex, partly below ground, is a teenagers' mecca. Open always. Shops: 10A.M. – 7P.M., closed Sunday, Monday morning. Métro: Châtelet, Les Halles.

Invalides. A 17th-century army veterans' hospital, home to the Army Museum and Napoleon's tomb. Open: Museum 10A.M. – 6P.M. (5P.M. October – March); Napoleon's tomb 10A.M. – 6P.M. (7P.M. June – August, 5P.M. October – March). Métro: Latour-Maubourg, Invalides.

La Madeleine. A Greco-Roman temple on the outside and a magnificent church inside. Open 7:30A.M. – 7P.M. (Sunday 8A.M. – 1:30P.M.; 3:30 – 7P.M.). Métro: Madeleine.

Notre-Dame Cathedral. A masterpiece of early Gothic and the symbol of Paris for 800 years. The view from the towers is superb, and the crypt reveals the Roman foundations of the city. Open 8A.M. – 7P.M. (Saturday 8A.M. – 12:30P.M., 2 – 7P.M.). Crypt 10A.M. – 6P.M. (5P.M. October – March). Métro: Cité, Maubert-Mutualité, Hôtel-de-Ville.

Sainte-Chapelle. A 13th-century jewel of Gothic architecture, with breathtaking stained glass. Open 9:30A.M. – 6:30P.M. (10A.M. – 5P.M., October – March). Métro: Cité.

Place des Vosges. The heart of the Marais, an elegant square of matching houses, planned by Henri IV in 1605. Victor Hugo lived at no. 6, now a museum. Métro: St-Paul, Chemin-Vert.

Paris has many parks and gardens for repose.

and ten years later it was the Nazis' last foothold in Paris.

Plumb in the centre, the 23 metre (75 foot) pink granite Obelisk of Luxor from the temple of Ramses II dates back to 1300 B.C. and was erected here in 1836. For a change, it's not something that Napoleon laid his hands on during a campaign, but was a gift from Mohammed Ali, viceroy of Egypt. The two imposing horses that watch over the opening to the Champs-Elysées are replicas of the great Chevaux de Marly, sculpted by Coustou between 1740 and 1745. (The marble originals now grace the Cour Marly of the Louvre.)

Jardin des Tuileries

After the bustle of the place de la Concorde and the Champs-Elysées, the Tuileries gardens, named after a 13th-century tileworks, provide a pleasant refuge among the chestnut trees and Maillol's sensual statues. The impressive size of the gardens results from the burning down of the Palais des Tuileries during the 1871 Commune (see page 21); a few fragments can be seen by the **Jeu de Paume** exhibition building in the northwest corner. Children can enjoy donkey rides, puppet shows in spring and summer, and model boats on the circular ponds.

In the corner near the Seine, facing place de la Concorde, the **Orangerie** is known for its two oval rooms with Monet's beautiful *Nymphéas* (waterlilies) murals, but don't miss the marvellous Impressionist and post-Impressionist paintings upstairs (see page 74).

At the eastern end of the Tuileries stands the pink **Arc de Triomphe du Carrousel**, started at roughly the same time but finished much more quickly than its bigger brother at l'Etoile, which is visible from here in a straight line beyond the obelisk in place de la Concorde. The same axis continues into the distant haze to the skyscrapers of La Défense and the Grande Arche.

Palais du Louvre

This is truly one of the world's treasure houses (see page 67 for more about the contents). Its harmonious lines are deceptive: the Louvre has been eight centuries in the making. Ever since Philippe Auguste built a fortress in 1190 to protect Paris from attack along the river, kings and queens have added to it and altered it. Louis XIV more or less abandoned the Louvre when he moved the court to Versailles, and it was taken over by artists, sculptors, and squatters. The Revolutionaries declared it to be a museum, and opened it to the public in 1793. As the home of the *Vénus de Milo* and

The big wheel is a summer fixture in the Tuileries gardens.

Mona Lisa, the Louvre drew ever-greater crowds, until by the beginning of the 1980s it was unable to cope. An enormous new reception area was excavated (revealing parts of the original fort). The controversial glass **pyramid** designed by I.M. Pei in the Cour Napoléon serves as the museum's main entrance and focus.

The old church of **Saint-Germain l'Auxerrois** on the eastern side of the complex dates from around 1200, but, like the palace, it was adapted many times, and often served as the royal chapel.

Seen from the little Arc de Triomphe du Carrousel, the pyramid marks the Louvre's main entrance.

Palais-Royal

The Palais-Royal, across the rue de Rivoli from the Louvre, was built as Cardinal Richelieu's residence in 1639 (it became "royal" when Anne of Austria moved in with young Louis XIV). This serene, arcaded palace, with its garden of lime trees and beeches — and the pond where Louis XIV nearly drowned — has had a colourful past. In the days of Philippe d'Orléans, Regent of France while Louis XV was a child, the Palais-Royal was the scene of notorious orgies. A later duke (another Philippe) constructed apartments round the garden, with two theatres (one became the national Comédie Française), shops, and cafés that soon attracted fashionable society. In the ferment that led up to the Revolution, it was a scene of furious debate. On 13 July 1789 a young firebrand orator, Camille Desmoulins, stood on a table at the Palais-Royal's Café de Foy to sound a call to arms. The Bastille was stormed the next day.

Giving himself the name Philippe Egalité (equality), the duke tried to curry favour with the Revolutionaries but was guillotined anyway. After the Revolution, the palace became a gambling den again and narrowly escaped destruction in the 1871 uprising. Once it was restored, between 1872 and 1876, the palace became respectable and today houses the Council of State and the Constitutional Council. Some of the shops still exist, and the sumptuously decorated Grand Véfour restaurant looks just the way it did 200 years ago.

The main quadrangle, the **Cour d'Honneur**, was filled in 1986 with rows of black-and-white striped stone columns by Daniel Buren. Some are short, some tall, a few are just the right height for sitting on.

Next to the Palais-Royal stand the **Banque de France**, east of the garden, and the **Bibliothèque Nationale** (National Library), just north of it. The idea of a royal library was born in 1368, when Charles V placed 973 manuscripts in the Louvre. Two centuries later, François I acquired new material, had Oriental, Latin, and Greek texts copied, and made it all available to scholars. He also ruled in 1573 that a copy of any work printed in France had to be given to the library. It has had to grow non-stop to house more than 10 million books, 12 million engravings, 650,000 maps, and more than 350,000 ancient manuscripts, one of which is Charlemagne's *Evangéliaire*. A new building on the Left Bank just opposite Bercy, dubbed *Très Grande Bibliothèque* (Very Large Library), now houses most of the enormous collection.

Les Halles

Les Halles, east of the Palais-Royal, this was for centuries the site of the capital's central food markets (now in a more spacious if less colourful location at Rungis, near Orly). To widespread regret, the great cast-iron and glass pavilions were torn down in the 1970s. They were eventually replaced by today's gardens and play areas, and the **Forum des Halles**, a maze-like shopping mall partly below ground. Saturdays bring throngs of teenagers from the suburbs to shop, watch films, roller skate, munch fast food, and generally hang out together. The liveliest meeting place in the area is the handsome Renaissance **Fontaine des Innocents** (once part of a cemetery). Bars, restaurants, and 24-hour brasseries line the adjoining rue Berger and the streets leading off it. Clubs and discos around here come alive at midnight and stay open to dawn, especially at weekends. It's not all innocent fun: drink and drugs mix with pickpockets and prostitutes. rue Saint-Denis, once known primarily as a red-light district, is now pedestrianized, but still has its share of sex shops.

The great church of **Saint-Eustache** dominates the north side of Les Halles. Built during the 16th and 17th centuries, the concept is late Gothic, the details are Renaissance, and the effect is awe-inspiring. Notice the sad modern shrine, with sculptures of the departing market traders, and the poem referring to a "paradise lost." If you are lucky, you may hear a recital on the splendid organ, or the choir rehearsing.

☛ Pompidou Centre (Beaubourg)

East of the Forum, streets closed to traffic and lined with cafés, brasseries, art galleries, and boutiques link up with the unusual Centre Georges Pompidou, housing the Musée National d'Art Moderne (see page 70). Controversy raged for years after the

1977 opening of this multi-coloured "oil refinery." The comparison came as no surprise to the architects, Italians Renzo Piano and Gianfranco Franchi and Englishman Richard Rogers, who deliberately left the building's service systems visible. Some 11,000 square metres (118,000 square feet) of glass, 15,000 tons of steel, and 41 escalators make up a structure 42 metres high and 166 metres long (135 feet by 543 feet).

The modern complex of Forum des Halles contrasts with the late-Gothic church of Saint-Eustache.

The sloping **plaza** outside is one of Paris' most popular locations for street performers. Any time until 10:00 P.M. you can take the free **escalators** that run in transparent tubes from the bottom left to the top right-hand corner and see Paris unfold before your eyes. Most of the Pompidou center is closed for extensive renovations and scheduled to reopen in 2000. The escalators will still be accessible, however.

Place Vendôme

Louis XIV wanted the perfect setting for a monument to himself. He found it in the square then known as the Hôtel Vendôme, and in 1699 a statue of the king on horseback was erected in the centre of the square. As for the surrounding houses, only Louis' financiers could afford the rents. Now, the Ministry of Justice shares the square with banks, famous jewellers, and the Ritz Hotel. Like all royal statues, that of Louis XIV was overthrown during the Revolution. Its replacement, the Vendôme column, is a spiral of bronze reliefs commemorating the victories of Napoleon, cast from 1,250 cannons captured from the Austrians at Austerlitz and topped by a statue of the emperor.

Opéra-Garnier and the Grands Boulevards

Window-shop your way past the goldsmiths and furriers of the rue de la Paix to the ornate opera house (now sporting the name of its architect Charles Garnier to distinguish it from the new Opéra-Bastille; see page 52). Begun at the height of Napoleon III's Second Empire when Paris was Europe's most glamorous capital, it was only completed in 1875, after the Commune. The public rooms and the staircase are in the grand manner — more so even than the auditorium, which holds a mere 2,000 spectators. Underneath the building is a small lake, which provided the inspiration for the phantom's hiding place in Paul Leroux's *Phantom of the Opera*. The vast false ceiling was painted by Chagall in 1964. Now the home of the national ballet company, Opéra-Garnier was renovated in 1995.

A stock exchange, the bank of France, a theatre: these were among the uses proposed for the huge neo-Classical church, **La Madeleine,** also renovated recently. Napoleon's instinct was to turn it into a temple of glory for his army, but his architect suggested the Arc de Triomphe instead. The restored monarchy opted for a church, as originally intended when building started under Louis XV, and it was finally consecrated in 1842. Climb the steps for a great view down the rue Royale to the place de la Concorde and National Assembly beyond.

The renovated Musée Jacqemart-André reopened in 1997 at 158 boulevard Haussmann, not far from La Madeleine. Housed in the superb mansion of 19th-century art collector Edouard André, the museum contains a superb collection of Italian Renaissance and 18th-century French paintings.

The **grands boulevards** running from the Madeleine past the Opéra and all the way to place de la Bastille were the fashionable heart of Paris from the 1860s until well into the 20th century. They have fallen somewhat out of favour since, but their majestic sweep can still evoke former glories. On the

The pediment of the church of La Madeleine illustrates the story of Christ and Mary Magdalene.

boulevard des Capucines, you can retrace the footsteps of Renoir, Manet, and Pissarro as they took their paintings to Nadar's house, at number 35, for the historic 1874 exhibition of Impressionism. Nowadays, the boulevards are the venue of a number of popular cinemas — appropriately enough, for it was at the Hôtel Scribe, near the Opéra, that the Lumière brothers staged the first public moving picture show in 1895.

Montmartre

Montmartre is the hilltop village, with its narrow, winding streets and dead-ends, which for the last 200 years has been associated with artists. The *Montmartrobus* spares you the walk and shows you some of the area in a single tour, but the best way to discover Montmartre at your own pace is to start early, and start at the top. Take the métro to Abbesses, use the elevator to the exit (the line runs deep below ground here), and as you leave notice the 1900 Art-Nouveau entrance, saved from another station. rue Yvonne le Tac leads to the base station of a funicular railway. It was here that St. Denis was martyred (see page 12) and where Saint Ignatius Loyola founded the Jesuit movement in 1534.

The funicular (it takes métro and bus tickets) climbs to the terrace in front of the Byzantine-style basilica of **Sacré-Cœur**. Standing at the highest point in Paris, it's one of the city's principal landmarks, and was for years one of the most controversial. Artists scorned it as a vulgar pastiche, and the working-class inhabitants of the area resented the way it was erected as a symbol of penitence for the insurrection of the 1871 Commune — they didn't feel penitent in the least. The Sacré-Cœur's conspicuous whiteness comes from the local Château-Landon limestone, which bleaches on contact with carbon dioxide in the air and hardens with age. For many, the most striking feature of the basilica is the view of the city from the dome or the terrace below.

Just a few steps to the west of Sacré-Cœur is **Saint-Pierre-de-Montmartre,** one of the city's oldest churches. Consecrated in 1147, 16 years before the church of Saint-Germain-des-Prés (see page 59), it is a significant work of early Gothic, belied by its 18th-century façade. The Sacré-Cœur's architect, Paul Abadie, wanted to demolish Saint-Pierre, but he was overruled, and it was restored "as a riposte to the Sacré-Cœur."

The nearby **place du Tertre** was once the centre of village life. Try to visit during the early morning — before the mass-

There has always been fierce argument over Sacré-Cœur, but no debate about the view.

production artists set up their easels and the crowds take over.

In place Emile Goudeau, just downhill, number 13 was the site of the studio known as the **Bateau-Lavoir** (so-called because the building resembled the laundry boats that used to travel along the Seine), before it was destroyed by fire. Here, if any one place was the birthplace of modern art: Picasso, Braque, and Juan Gris developed Cubism; Modigliani painted in a style all his own; and Apollinaire wrote his first surrealistic verses. Some of their predecessors — Renoir, van Gogh, and Gauguin — once lived and worked just north of place du Tertre in rue Cortot, rue de l'Abreuvoir, and rue Saint-Rustique.

On the rue Saint-Vincent at the corner of rue des

Visit place du Tertre early, before the artists set up their easels and the crowds arrive.

Saules, look out for Paris' last surviving **vineyard**, the tiny Clos de Montmartre. Then wind your way down rue Lepic, a market street lined with marvellous food shops. Suddenly, at place Blanche, everything changes. You hit boulevard Clichy, or it hits you. Right on the corner is the Moulin Rouge, still staging its nightly cabarets, mostly to package tours. All the way east to **place Pigalle** and beyond runs a ribbon of tawdry night-life, with countless sex shops, peep shows, and other dubious attractions, punctuated by a few conventional restaurants and bars. By evening, tour buses from all over Europe are parked nose to tail in the street. Later on, it's worth avoiding the métro here unless you want to share it with reeling drunks.

The principal **cemetery** of Montmartre, where luminaries of the arts such as the composers Berlioz and Offenbach lie buried, may seem a world away, but it's only a short walk west from the Moulin Rouge to the entrance (west past the Moulin Rouge, then right at avenue Rachel.

The Marais

The district to the north of Ile de la Cité and Ile Saint-Louis has bravely withstood the onslaught of modern construction. It provides a remarkably authentic record of the development of the city, from the reign of Henri IV at the end of the 16th century to the advent of the Revolution. Built on reclaimed marshland, as its name suggests, the Marais contains some of Europe's most elegant Renaissance mansions (*hôtels*), many of which now serve as museums and libraries. The Marais has

Side by side in the Père Lachaise cemetery, the tombs of La Fontaine and Molière.

Cemeteries

It's curiously calming to wander among the many tall tombs, packed together like rows of stone beach huts. Free maps of Paris cemeteries (usually available at the entrance) help you to seek out the graves of the great.

Cimetière du Père Lachaise, northeast of place de la Bastille, has seen an estimated 1,350,000 burials since its foundation in 1804. It even served as a battleground in 1871, when the Communards made a last stand. The Mur des Fédérés in the southeast corner marks the place where many were executed by firing squad. Celebrity tombs include those of the painter Ingres, dancer Isadora Duncan, composers Rossini and Chopin, who made Paris their home, writers such as La Fontaine, Molière, Balzac, Proust, and Oscar Wilde, his tomb marked by a fine monument by Jacob Epstein. More recent arrivals are Yves Montand, Simone Signoret, and Jim Morrison of The Doors, who died mysteriously in Paris in 1971.

The tranquil **Cimetière de Montmartre**, below the hill, has an equally illustrious roll-call: Berlioz (buried with Harriet Smithson, who inspired his *Symphonie Fantastique*), Offenbach, Degas, Feydeau, Nijinsky, the great chef Carème, film-maker François Truffaut, and Louise Weber, credited with inventing the cancan.

In the **Montparnasse** cemetery, you can find the tombs of composers Saint-Saëns and César Franck, writer Maupassant and poet Baudelaire, Dreyfus, the Jewish officer whose conviction for spying split the nation, André Citroën, the car maker, Pierre Laval, the collaborationist Vichy prime minister (executed while dying from a suicide attempt), and philosopher Jean-Paul Sartre, who spent much of his later life on the Left Bank.

Beneath Montparnasse, the subterranean **Catacombs** are old quarries whose corridors were used in the past for the reburial of millions of skeletons removed from overcrowded cemeteries and charnel houses. Unidentified, they are stacked on shelves, piled in heaps, or artfully arranged into macabre patterns. It's cold, damp, and morbid, but if skulls and bones appeal, find the main entrance in place Denfert-Rochereau (shortened to Denfert, it sounds just like the old name, *Place d'Enfer*, Hell Square).

become fashionable again and trendy boutiques seem to spring up daily.

Take the métro to Rambuteau and start at the corner of the rue des Archives and rue des Francs-Bourgeois, named after the poor (not *bourgeois* at all) allowed to live here tax-free in the 14th century. The national archives are stored in an 18th-century mansion, the **Hôtel de Soubise**. Across a vast, horseshoe-shaped courtyard, you come across the exquisite Rococo style of Louis XV's time, in the apartments of the Prince and Princess of Soubise. Up on the first floor is the **Musée de l'Histoire de France**, with gems such as the only known portrait of Joan of Arc painted in her lifetime and the diary kept by Louis XVI. His entry for 14 July 1789, the day the Bastille was stormed, reads *Rien* (Nothing).

A garden (not always open to the public) connects the Hôtel de Soubise with its twin, the **Hôtel de Rohan**, on the rue Vieille du Temple. Look out for Robert le Lorrain's fine *Les Chevaux d'Apollon*, over the old stables in the second courtyard, widely considered to be the most beautiful 18th-century sculpture in France.

Also on the rue des Francs-Bourgeois, the Hôtel Carnavalet was the home of the lady of letters, Madame de Sévigné. Now it houses the **Musée Carnavalet** (see page 75). The **Musée Picasso**, nearby at 5 rue Thorigny, is housed in the beautifully restored Hôtel Salé (see page 71).

The rue des Francs-Bourgeois ends at the loveliest residential square in Paris, **place des Vosges**. Henri IV had it laid out in 1605 on the site of an old horse-market, his idea (borrowed from Catherine de Médici) being to have "all the houses in the same symmetry." After the wedding festivities of his son Louis XIII were held here, the gardens became the fashionable place to promenade, and later a spot for aristocratic duels. Today there's a children's playground, and the rest is perfect for just sitting.

The best time to see the square is in the winter, when the chestnut trees are bare and don't obscure the pink brick and honey-coloured stone façades. Victor Hugo, author of *Les Misérables*, lived at number 6, now a museum housing many of his manuscripts, artefacts, and wonderful drawings.

While in the Marais, take a wander round the old **Jewish quarter** (or *shtetl*, as the Paris Jews call it), especially if you are looking for somewhere unusual to eat. Jews have lived around the **rue des Rosiers** for centuries, and the rue Ferdinand Duval was known until 1900 as the rue des Juifs. The other main street, rue des Ecouffes (me-

Sun or shade? The arcades of the place des Vosges have sheltered Parisians for centuries.

dieval slang for moneylenders), completes the lively shopping area, with delicatessens, kosher butchers, and even kosher pizza shops. More recent arrivals from the Jewish communities of North Africa have replaced the Ashkenazim of Eastern Europe, who themselves took the place of the Sephardim who first settled in Paris in the 13th century.

Bastille

The large, circular **place de la Bastille** is enjoying a new lease on life. No trace remains of the prison stormed in 1789:

even the column in the centre commemorates a later revolution, that of 1830. Long a run-down area, it was given a shot in the arm by the construction of the **Opéra-Bastille**, one of former President Mitterrand's great projects. This opened in 1990 to a chorus of hostile comment. Modernists attacked Carlos Ott's building as being too timid, conservatives said it was an ugly misfit. At least the acoustics were rated a success, and soon the new home of the National Opera became part of the cultural life of Paris. Take a tour and try to go to a performance. In the adjacent streets, such as rue de la Couronne, traditional old shops alternate with art galleries, artists' studios and restaurants. Just to the northeast of the Opéra in rue de la Main d'Or, rue de Lappe, and their offshoots, clubs and discos have revived an old night-life tradition.

LEFT BANK

The Left Bank (*rive gauche*) does its best to live up to a bohemian and intellectual image gained centuries ago. There is much more to the Left Bank than the student life of the Latin Quarter, but so many schools and colleges are packed into a small area that it's the young who set the pace. Writers and artists used to meet in the cafés of Saint-Germain-des-Prés: today's equivalent are the media people, film directors, and journalists who still do, although the atmosphere is touristy. Montparnasse took over from Montmartre as the haunt of the avant-garde in the 1920s and still stakes a claim. The Left Bank has monuments and museums, too, and many Parisians rate the Luxembourg Gardens as their favourite park.

Latin Quarter

As far back as the 13th century, when Paris's first university moved from the cloisters of Notre-Dame to the Left Bank, the young came to the *quartier*, originally to learn Latin.

Here, the spirit of inquiry has traditionally been nurtured, sometimes leading to protest and outright revolt before subsiding into lifelong scepticism.

In ancient days the university simply meant a collection of scholars who met on a street corner, in a public square, or courtyard to listen to a lecture given from a bench or balcony. Now open-air discussions may be held over coffee on some café terrace on the boulevard Saint-Michel, or in the streets around the faculty buildings of the Sorbonne and other schools. Among the institutes of learning located here are France's two most famous lycées, Henri IV and Louis le Grand, where a large number of France's future élite are taught.

> **French friends exchange kisses on alternate cheeks, and not just two, but three, four, or more.**

Life on the Left Bank with a difference — houseboats floating on the Seine.

The Left Bank's little church of Saint-Séverin is celebrated for its stonework and stained glass.

Begin your visit to the Latin Quarter at the **place Saint-Michel**, where students still come to buy their books and stationery, or to gather round the bombastic 1860s fountain by Davioud, one of the great Paris meeting places. Plunge into the narrow streets of the **Saint-Séverin** quarter to the east (rue Saint-Séverin, rue de la Harpe, and rue Galande). You will discover a medieval world updated by the varied exotica of smoky Greek barbecues, Tunisian pastry shops, and a wealth of other eating establishments.

Little **Saint-Julien-le-Pauvre**, one of the oldest churches in Paris, dating from between 1165 and 1220, is a jewel of early Gothic architecture and now hosts chamber and religious music concerts. With its wafting incense and its masses said in Greek or Arabic (the church belongs to the Melchite sect of the Greek Orthodox Church), Saint-Julien is not out of place in an area packed with Middle Eastern restaurants. Just across rue Saint-Jacques stands the exquisite 13th- to 15th-century Flamboyant Gothic **church of Saint-Séverin**, in which Dante is said to have prayed and Saint-Saëns asked to be honorary organist.

The Sorbonne

Named after the 13th-century college for theological students established by Robert de Sorbon, the university was later taken in hand by Cardinal Richelieu, who financed its reconstruction (1624–1642). Few of the rather forbidding buildings are open to the public, but you can go inside the 17th-century **courtyard** with its ornate sundial and see the outside of the Baroque library and domed church. Protest against overcrowding, antiquated teaching, bureaucracy, and the very basis of the social system made the Sorbonne a focal point for unrest in 1968, a year of ferment throughout Europe. When the police invaded the sanctuary — which for centuries had guaranteed student immunity — the revolt exploded onto the streets. Students and workers made common cause, and there followed widespread national strikes which threatened the survival of the government. (Over in the quiet, tree-shaded **place de la Sorbonne** it all seems a long time ago.) In the aftermath of the revolts, the Sorbonne was absorbed into the huge Paris Universities monolith and lost its independence.

Standing virtually opposite the Sorbonne's rue des Ecoles entrance, at 6 place Paul-Painlevé, are the massive brick ruins of the ancient Roman public baths. They survived as part of an abbey — now the **Musée National du Moyen Age**, still often called by its former name, Musée de Cluny (see page 75). Its most famous exhibits are the wonderful 15th-century **tapestries**, the *Lady with the Unicorn*.

Panthéon

A stroll up the rue Saint-Jacques past the most famous high school in Paris, the Lycée Louis le Grand, will bring you to the gigantic neo-Classical **Panthéon**. Designed for Louis XV as the church of Sainte-Geneviève (1755), it was secularized during the Revolution to serve as a mausoleum. For most of the 19th century the Panthéon oscillated between secular and consecrated status, according to the current régime's political colour. Finally Victor Hugo's funeral in 1885 settled the issue in favour of a secular mausoleum. He was followed by realist writer Emile Zola, socialist leader Jean Jaurès, Léon Gambetta (leader during the 1870 siege of Paris), Louis Braille (inventor of the blind alphabet), Pierre and Marie Curie (discoverers of radium), and many others.

The empty interior is sterile, however, its windows covered by huge, late-19th-century paintings. The crypt is even more dispiriting, a grim maze of corridors lined with cells containing the tombs of the famous, as well as many whom few will have heard of. A good display on the history of the Panthéon is the best part of the visit.

Escape to the old streets behind the Panthéon, where the bustling **rue Mouffetard** and its offshoots are more like a village than part of Paris. The stalls of the morning market (see page 85) are piled with superb produce. Here and in the tiny place de la Contrescarpe you will find a large choice of ethnic restaurants, especially Thai, Vietnamese, and Chinese.

Bakers start work long before dawn, producing works of art that appeal to all the senses.

A block to the east is where signs to **Arènes de Lutèce** lead you to a little park, site of a Roman amphitheatre, restored after its remains were found during the 19th century.

Jardin du Luxembourg

Bright with flowers, scattered with statues of famous characters, the Luxembourg Gardens are the prettiest green space on the Left Bank. Students find quiet corners to read or relax; children can sail their boats on the octagonal pond or ride a merry-go-round designed by none other than Charles Garnier, architect of the Opéra (see page 44), and old men meet under the chestnut trees to play chess or a game of *boules*. The Palais du Luxembourg, built for Marie de Médici early in the 17th century, now houses the French Senate.

East along the Seine

Back down by the Seine, but heading eastwards, stroll past the Jussieu University complex that stands on the site of the Halles aux Vins (wine market). The **Institut du Monde Arabe** (Arab World Institute), at 23 quai Saint-Bernard, was built with the help of 16 Arab nations to foster cultural links between the Islamic world and the West. The fine museum inside traces the cultures of the Arab world, both the pre-Islamic and Islamic periods, with superb exhibits. The best way to see them is to start on the 7th floor and work down. A library of over 40,000 volumes covers all aspects of Arab culture. The rooftop restaurant's menu includes every Middle Eastern dish you could think of.

The **Jardin des Plantes** next door, created by Louis XIII as "a royal garden of medicinal plants," is still an excellent botanical and decorative garden, with exotic plants in the hothouses. The adjoining **Musée d'Histoire Naturelle**, with armies of skeletons, butterflies, and mineral samples, is resolutely old-fashioned.

The vast grey **Ministère de l'Economie et des Finances,** with one foot in the water on the other side of the Seine, is part of the conspicuous redevelopment of the Bercy district, including a new bridge, Pont Charles de Gaulle.

Saint-Germain-des-Prés

This Left Bank area is one of the most attractive neighbourhoods in all Paris. Not part of the Latin Quarter, but rather an extension of it, this is the home of numerous publishing houses, the Académie Française, expensive interior design and fashion shops, bookshops to suit all tastes, and café terraces designed for people-watching. It used to be the headquarters of Jean-Paul Sartre and his existentialist acolytes who would wear, winter or summer, black corduroys and long woollen scarves. In place Saint-Germain-des-Prés, the Café Bonaparte on the north side and the Deux Magots on the west provide ring-side seats for a street theatre of mimes,

The Luxembourg Gardens are the Left Bank's loveliest park. The Senate meets in the Palace.

musicians, and neighbourhood eccentrics. The Café de Flore round the corner has hung on to its intellectual tradition more than the others, perhaps because of its rather ideologically confused history. It has been home successively to the extreme right Action Française group under Charles Maurras in 1899, the poet and surrealist precursor Apollinaire in 1914 (who, with his friends, liked to provoke brawls), and then Sartre's existentialists during the 1950s, a peaceful bunch who never got enough sleep to have the energy to fight.

Also on the place Saint-Germain stands the **church of Saint-Germain-des-Prés**, the oldest in Paris. It is a mixture of Romanesque and Gothic, with a clock-tower dating from about the year 1000 and a 17th-century porch sheltering 12th-century doorposts. The interior was restored after the Revolutionaries gutted it and used it as a gunpowder factory. The church is a wonderful venue for frequent concerts.

To the north of the square the rue Bonaparte leads the way past the **Ecole Nationale Supérieure des Beaux-Arts** (Fine Arts School). This structure incorporates fragments of medieval and Renaissance architecture and sculpture that make it a living museum. During the events of May 1968, it became something of a poster factory.

The very august **Palais de l'Institut de France**, home of the Académie Française, is on the quai de Conti by the Pont des Arts. Designed by Louis le Vau in 1668 to harmonize with the Louvre across the river, the Institut began as a school for the sons of provincial gentry, financed by a legacy of Cardinal Mazarin. Then in 1805 the building was turned over to the Institut, which comprises the Académie Française — the supreme arbiter of the French language founded by Cardinal Richelieu in 1635 — and the académies des Belles-Lettres, Sciences, Beaux-Arts, and Sciences Morales et Politiques. Guides to the Institut like to point out the east pavilion, site of the old 14th-century Tour de Nesle. They say that Queen Jeanne de Bourgogne used the tower to watch out for likely young lovers, whom she summoned for the night and then had thrown into the Seine.

Montparnasse

Don't go looking for a hill: the Mount Parnassus was a mound left after quarrying, and has long since been removed. This is the quarter where they invented the cancan in 1845, at the Grande Chaumière dancehall (now defunct). In the twenties, Montparnasse took over from Montmartre as the stamping ground of the city's artistic colony, or at least its avant-garde, as Picasso moved over. Expatriates such as Hemingway, Gertrude Stein, F. Scott Fitzgerald, and John dos Passos also took to the free-living atmosphere and added to the mystique themselves. The attraction isn't immediately evident: the wide, straight **boulevard du Montparnasse** is plain by Paris standards. Nowadays, the majority of the haunts where the Lost Generation found itself have been polished and painted, or even entirely rebuilt, but plenty of people think it worth paying the elevated prices to feel they might be sitting in a seat once warmed by Modigliani, Lenin, or Sartre.

The tall (59-storey), black **Tour Montparnasse** may be an egregious eyesore, but the view from the top is marvellous (33 avenue du Maine, open daily 9:30 A.M.-10:00 P.M.).

The **cemetery** (see page 49) to the east of the station, reached from boulevard Edgar Quinet, is the resting place of some famous and controversial figures in French history.

Invalides

Geographically if not temperamentally part of the Left Bank, the Palais-Bourbon is the seat of the **Assemblée Nationale** (parliament). It makes a stately riverside façade for the 7th *ar-*

Cafés with a Past

Many of the cafés once frequented by great artists and thinkers still flourish — although today's prices might come as a shock.

St. Germain-des-Prés. Camus, Sartre, and Simone de Beauvoir used to meet at *Les Deux Magots* at 170 blvd. St-Germain, 75006. Now it's something of a tourist show year round (closed August). Another favourite was *Café de Flore*, right next door (closed July). *Le Procope*, 13 rue de l'Ancienne Comédie, 75006, was the first coffee-house in Paris, dating from 1686; it's said that Voltaire drank 40 cups a day here, and that the young Napoleon had to leave his hat as security while he went for money to pay the bill; now it's just a restaurant, with good value, fixed-price menus.

Montparnasse. One of Henry Miller's hang-outs, *Le Select* (99 blvd. du Montparnasse, 75006) opened as an all-night bar in 1925; les Six, the group of composers including Erik Satie and Francis Poulenc, met here. *La Coupole* opposite (102 blvd. du Montparnasse, 75014) was a favourite with Sartre and de Beauvoir in the years after World War II; it has been rebuilt and now seats 400. *Le Dôme* at number 108 has lost some of its character since the days of Modigliani and Stravinsky, with elaborate remodelling. Across the street, Picasso, Derain, and Vlaminck used to meet at the *Rotonde* (105 blvd. du Montparnasse, 75006). At the junction of boulevard du Montparnasse and boulevard Saint-Michel, *La Closerie des Lilas* is where Lenin and Trotsky plotted before the Russian Revolution, and where Hemingway and his buddies met after World War I.

Right bank. The resplendent Café de la Paix in Le Grand Hôtel at 12 blvd. des Capucins, 75009 (see page 141) was a favourite with the Prince of Wales (later Edward VII) and Oscar Wilde, Zola, and Maupassant; Caruso also used to dine here after singing at the Opéra across the street. Near Les Halles, La Promenade de Vénus at 44 rue du Louvre, 75001, was the 1920s headquarters of André Breton and his fellow surrealists. Market workers and celebrities used to share the 24-hour Au Pied de Cochon (At the Pig's Foot), 6 rue Coquillière, 75001 (see page 141). In the Marais, Lenin and Trotsky (again) met at La Tartine, 24 rue de Rivoli, 75004, a dark little local bar at the unfashionable end of this long street.

rondissement, with its 18th-century embassies, ministries, and private mansions (*hôtels particuliers*). Napoleon added the Grecian columns facing the Pont de la Concorde; the more graceful character of the Palais-Bourbon is seen from its entrance on the south side. Designed for a daughter of Louis XIV in 1722, it can be entered only on written request or as the guest of a deputy. If you do get in, look for the Delacroix paintings in the library, illustrating the history of civilization.

The Prime Minister's splendid residence, at 57 rue de Varenne, is a short walk from the National Assembly. Its private park has a music pavilion favoured for secret strategy sessions. The same quiet 18th-century street holds the **Rodin Museum** at number 77, in the delightful Hôtel Biron (see page 75).

The most important sight in the area, however, is the monumentally impressive **Hôtel des Invalides**, which was established by Louis XIV as the first national hospital and retirement home for soldiers wounded during action. At one time it housed approximately 6,000 veterans, but Napoleon took over part of it to form the **Musée de l'Armée** (Army Museum), which still occupies a large proportion. Then the Invalides came to symbolize the glory of Napoleon himself, when his remains were finally brought back from St. Helena in 1840 for burial in the chapel under the golden **Dôme**. His son, given the title of King of Rome when a baby, is buried in the crypt.

The main courtyard allows access to the adjoining church of **Saint-Louis-des-Invalides**, decorated with flags taken by French armies in battle since Waterloo. The courtyard itself contains the 18 cannon, including eight taken from Vienna, which Napoleon ordered to be fired on great occasions — including the birth of his son in 1811. The cannon sounded again for the 1918 Armistice and the funeral of Marshal Foch in 1929.

Just on the southwest corner of the Invalides is the **Ecole Militaire,** where officers have trained since the middle of the 18th century. Their former parade ground, the vast **Champ de Mars**, is now a green park stretching all the way to the Eiffel Tower. Horseraces were held here in the 1780s, and also five World Fairs between 1867 and 1937. In the 20th century it has become the front lawn of the Left Bank's most luxurious residences.

Eiffel Tower

Right from the start, it was a resounding success. In 1889, 2 million visitors paid 5 francs a head to climb to the top, and the figures have shown consistently that, whatever its critics may have said, the tower has its place in Paris's landscape.

Some monuments celebrate heroes, commemorate victories, honour kings or saints. This is a monument for its own sake. Its construction for the World Fair of 1889 was an astounding engineering achievement — some 15,000 pieces of metal joined by 2,500,000 rivets, soaring 320 metres (984 feet) into the sky on a base only 130 metres (430 feet) across. At the time, it was the tallest structure in the world. It also provided

Rodin's "Thinker" in the garden of the Rodin Museum, with the dome of Les Invalides in the background.

the perfect perch for transmitters when radio and TV came along.

On the tower's inauguration, the lifts were not yet in operation and Prime Minister Tirard stopped at the first platform (57 metres or 187 feet up), leaving his Minister of Commerce to go all the way to the top to present Gustave Eiffel with the Legion of Honour medal. Conceived purely as a temporary structure for the Fair, the tower was slated for destruction in 1910, but nobody had the heart to take it down. When new spotlights were installed in 1985 to illuminate the tower from within, even detractors had to admit that it did have something.

An audio-visual show about the tower is screened on the first platform; there are restaurants on the first and second, and a bar on the third. On a pollution-free day you can see for approximately 65 km (40 miles) from the top, but more often the view is clearer from the second platform. Try to get there an hour before sunset for the best light.

Pleasure boats and working barges alike tie up at the Port de Suffren, near the Eiffel Tower.

WESTERN OUTSKIRTS

Bois de Boulogne

The chic 16th *arrondissement* is bordered on its west side by the Bois de Boulogne, the capital's biggest park, 900 hectares (2,200 acres) of green space, lakes, and woodland. The remnant of an old hunting forest, it was tamed by Baron Haussmann into resembling a London park. The **Bagatelle**, once a royal retreat, has a very lovely English garden, bursting with flowers during spring and early summer. The **Jardin d'Acclimatation** is an amusement park with plenty of attractions for children: shows, rides, and a small zoo. There are bikes for rent outside its entrance for exploring the rest of the Bois. The **Musée des Arts et Traditions Populaires** has excellent displays of folk arts and crafts through the ages. Also within the park are a boating lake and two fine racecourses, Longchamp for flat races and Auteuil for steeplechases. *Warning*: in spite of police patrols, after dark parts of the Bois de Boulogne are reckoned to be the most dangerous places in Paris.

La Défense

As you follow the long avenue de la Grande-Armée leaving from l'Etoile, the battery of towers grows bigger and bigger as you approach through the elegant, leafy suburb of Neuilly. Cross the river and there you are: in a mini-Manhattan that has grown by fits and starts since 1969 to become a city in its own right. In the process, it has somehow managed to get a soul, in spite of the inhuman scale of some of its windswept spaces.

The Grande Arche is farther away than most of the towers, and only when you get close do you realize just how big it is. A hollow cube 110 metres high and 106 metres wide (360 by 347 feet), it's broad enough to straddle the Champs-Elysées and high enough for Notre-Dame to fit underneath. Built with remarkable speed (Danish architect Johann-Otto von Sprekelsen won the contest in 1983 and it was ready for the bicentenary of the French Revolution in 1989), the Grande Arche lies directly in line with the Arc de Triomphe and the Cour Carrée of the Louvre. Its white gables are clothed in Carrara marble, the outer façades with a combination of grey marble and glass; the inside walls are covered with aluminium.

The two "legs" contain offices, while the roof houses conference rooms and exhibition space. Bubble lifts whisk you up through a fibreglass and Teflon "cloud," held by steel cables that stretch from one wall to the other, but the ride to the top is expensive and the view not much more striking than from the terrace.

The curious visiting crowds as well as the thousands who work here have encouraged the opening of more and more shops, cinemas, hotels, and restaurants. One of the cinemas, near the Grande Arche, has a big wraparound IMAX screen, and in the same building the **Musée de l'Automobile** displays over 100 classic cars, restored to mint condition.

The Grande Arche de la Défense could straddle the full width of the Champs-Elysées.

Across the main concourse a 12-metre (39-foot) bronze thumb by César sticks out like, well, a sore thumb. Stroll down the tiers of terraces and you'll find many more statues, fountains, and murals by Miró, Calder, and other modern artists, all detailed on street-plans given out at information desks.

MAJOR MUSEUMS

THE LOUVRE — Far less daunting and stuffy since its
facelift, the Musée du Louvre is still formidable for its sheer
size. In 1793, when the leaders of the Revolution declared
the palace a national museum, the Louvre held 630 works of
art; a recent inventory listed 250,000. Don't be put off — it's
an exhilarating experience just attempting to come to grips
with such vast collections of painting and sculpture, with ar-
tifacts from 5000 B.C. to 1848 (the date at which the Musée
d'Orsay takes over).

Whatever you might think of it, the glass **pyramid** designed by American architect I.M. Pei provides a striking
modern entrance. You descend by escalator to the reception
area, which comprises shops, cafés, and the ticket office. At
the information counter, collect a copy of the free **handbook**
with colour-coded floor plans. (Admission, too, is free on the
first Sunday of every month.)

Broad corridors lead to the various parts of the museum. The
museum authorities have made heroic efforts to help you find
your way through the labyrinth. Each of the three main wings
is named after one of France's great figures: the Richelieu
wing, the Sully wing in the east, and the Denon wing beside the
Seine. Each wing is then divided into numbered areas, which
are shown on the colour floor
plans. The locations of some
of the most famous exhibits
are pin-pointed. You *will* get
lost at times, but in doing so
you may discover unlooked-for marvels.

> *Entrée* – entrance
> *Sortie* – exit
> *Interdiction de photographier*
> – no cameras allowed

A good way to tackle the museum is to spend an initial
half-day seeing the highlights. For this, you may find an
acoustiguide (recorded tour) helpful. Look out for some of
the following highlights.

Medieval moat: The 12th-century fortress' foundations and drawbridge support.

Egyptian: The lion-headed *Sekhmet* (1400 B.C.) and the huge *Amenophis IV* (1370 B.C.).

Greek: The winged *Victory of Samothrace* and beautifully proportioned *Vénus de Milo*.

Italian: The splendid sculpture of the *Two Slaves* by Michelangelo; Leonardo da Vinci's fabled *Mona Lisa* (*La Joconde*), and also his sublime *Virgin of the Rocks*; Titian's voluptuous *Woman at her Toilet*; the poignant *Old Man and His Grandson* by Ghirlandaio.

French: Poussin's *Arcadian Shepherds*; Watteau's hypnotically melancholy *Gilles* and graceful *Embarkation for Cythera*; Fragonard's erotic *Le Verrou* (*The Bolt*); Delacroix's *Liberty Guiding the People;* and Courbet's piercing study of provincial bourgeoisie, *Funeral at Ornans*.

Dutch and Flemish: Rembrandt's cheerful *Self-Portrait with a Toque*, his beloved *Hendrickje Stoffels*, also portrayed

The glass pyramid creates a focus for the Louvre and lights its underground reception area.

nude in *Bathesheba Bathing*; Van Dyke's gracious, dignified *Charles I of England*; among scores of Rubens, his tender *Helena Fourment*.

Spanish: The uncompromising Velázquez portrait of *Queen Marianna of Austria*; El Greco's mystic *Christ on the Cross*; Ribera's gruesomely good-humoured *The Club Foot* (*Le Pied-Bot*).

German: A gripping *Self-Portrait* by Dürer; Holbein's *Erasmus*.

English: *Conversation in a Park* by Gainsborough.

MUSÉE D'ORSAY — "The station is superb and truly looks like a Fine Arts Museum, and since the Fine Arts Museum resembles a station, I suggest ... we make the change while we still can," joked the painter Edouard Detaille in 1900. In 1986 that was more or less what happened. Facing the Tuileries gardens across the river, the converted 19th-century hotel-cum-railway station was transformed into the impressive Musée d'Orsay, devoted to French art from 1848 to 1914. In effect, it carries on where the Louvre leaves off. Keeping the exterior much as it was, Italian architect Gae Aulenti adapted the interior to house many of the previously scattered works of that period, including the magnificent Impressionist collections formerly held in the Jeu de Paume. Sculpture is well represented, and photography is present from its inception (1839).

The d'Orsay is one of the easiest of great museums to navigate: the free floor plan is crystal clear, and so are the signs. There are mesmerizing arrays of work by Renoir, Cézanne, Manet, Monet (including five of his studies of Rouen Cathedral in various lights), and van Gogh (the best collection outside the van Gogh Museum in Amsterdam, with several of the pictures from his frenzied period of activity in the months before his death in 1890).

Both layout and lighting are astonishing; every part of the old terminus has been used in a highly imaginative way, and frequent lectures, guided tours, and concerts are scheduled. When you need a break, there is a café high up behind a huge clock, and on the middle level the former station hotel's restaurant, beautifully restored, is a restaurant again. It's worth noting, too, that the Musée d'Orsay is one of few Paris museums that is air-conditioned, and is thus a refreshing retreat on a hot day.

CENTRE GEORGES POMPIDOU (BEAUBOURG) — "That'll get them screaming," said the President of the time, Georges Pompidou, as he approved the plans (chosen from 681 competing designs) for the Centre National de l'Art Contemporain, later named Centre Georges Pompidou and occasionally known as Beaubourg after its 13th-century neighbourhood.

Its combination of public library, children's workshop and special library, *cinémathèque*, industrial design centre, and a music laboratory has made the complex a constant hive of activity, with free shows and a rendezvous point outside. The excellent **National Museum of Modern Art** on the 4th and then 3rd floors (in that order, and simple to follow with the free map) provides a rewarding education in all the disparate art movements of the 20th century, from the Fauve to Cubism to Abstract Expressionism, Dadaism, Surrealism, and all the breakaway factions and reactions which followed them. The great innovators are all here: Matisse, Picasso, Kandinsky, Léger, Dubuffet, Pollock, and sculptors Brancusi, Arp, and Giacommetti.

The 3rd floor takes up the story of ever-increasing fragmentation and experiment, and continues it almost to the present day. The 5th floor stages temporary exhibition; there's also a restaurant with a wonderful view. Unfortunately, until ongoing renovations are completed in 2000, you will have to confine your viewing to the exterior and the observation terrace on the top floor, reached by dramatic escalators.

MUSÉE DE L'ORANGERIE — A pavilion in the corner of the Tuileries gardens is home to the outstanding Jean Walther-Paul Guillaume Collection. By the terms of their wills, the legacy had to stay here, otherwise it might have been moved to the Musée d'Orsay. Masterpieces by Cézanne, Renoir, Utrillo, Rousseau, Modigliani, Picasso, Derain, and Soutine hang in the upstairs rooms. Guillaume himself knew most of the artists and several of them did portraits of him. The walls of the two oval rooms downstairs

The Musée d'Orsay is a fitting exhibition space for some of the world's best-known works of art.

are almost completely covered by huge murals of waterlilies (*Nymphéas*), which Monet painted as a gift to the nation.

MUSÉE PICASSO — Over 200 paintings, 158 sculptures, and hundreds of drawings, engravings, ceramics, and models for stage sets and costumes from Picasso's private collections were given to the nation by his heirs, in lieu of taxes owed on his death. The museum includes the artist's own collection of works by fellow painters Braque, Matisse, Miró, Degas, Renoir, and Rousseau. In addition, a number of intriguing private relics are displayed: letters, photo albums, bullfight

The inside-out design of the Pompidou Centre creates a fine backdrop for street performers.

tickets, and holiday post-cards.

MUSÉE NATIONAL DU MOYEN AGE (MUSÉE DE CLUNY) — The setting is amazing, an old abbey which incorporated the massive remains of the city's third-century Roman baths, the Thermes de Cluny. One of the exhibits is older still: the fragments of a monument to Jupiter (probably first century A.D.) discovered near Notre-Dame. Twenty-one of the 28 heads of the kings of Judah from Notre-Dame (see page 31) were found in a bank vault and are now here — notice that some retain traces of colouring. But the most celebrated treasures of all at this museum are without a doubt the late 15th-century **tapestries**, especially the set known as the *Lady with the Unicorn*, depicting the five senses.

PARC DE LA VILLETTE: CITÉ DES SCIENCES — If there's one thing this institution dislikes, it's being called a museum. First, the Parc de la Villette offers a whole range of activities, and second, it puts the accent firmly on participation. But as with any good museum, you can learn a lot and enjoy yourself too. There's something for all ages, and for anyone ready to be excited by the world of science.

The main building has a lot in common with Beaubourg, — although this one is four times bigger. A variety of themes are explored: space, health, communications, agriculture, etc. Some of the hands-on displays are fun, but you need to understand French to follow all the information presented.

The sizeable stainless-steel Géode sphere, made of 6,433 reflecting triangles, houses a cinema with a 360° movie screen 36 metres (118 feet) in diameter. As you watch the film, you feel as if you're part of it. There's also a 60-seat space-flight simulator. The principal exhibition area, the planetarium and aquarium, and the submarine *Argonaute* are covered by the entry fee (or Museum Pass), but all other activities — even the creative play areas for young children — cost extra and are fairly expensive. (See also page 75.)

A canal passes right through the park, so you can reach La Villette by boat from central Paris (a three-hour trip; see page 25). The nearby **Cité de la Musique**, on the other side of the canal, has a new concert hall, the ultra modern buildings of the Conservatoire National (music academy), and an impressively large rock venue, the Zénith.

The park is at its liveliest in the summer, when music festivals and the popular *Ciné-ma en Plein Air* (outdoor cinema) take place. You can obtain a complete schedule of events from the tourist office on the Champs-Elysées.

The finely detailed Lady with the Unicorn tapestries are works of intriguing symbolism.

EXCURSIONS

CHARTRES — Built around the year 1200, Chartres Cathedral is visible from far

Museums

Entry charges range from 25 to 50F. In some museums, those under 18 enter free, with those 18-25 and over 60 paying half price. In others, under 7 are free, 7-17 and students pay a reduced rate. Some museums charge less on Sundays.

The **Museum Pass** (*Carte Musées et Monuments*) gives entry to 65 museums and monuments in Paris and its region, including the Louvre and Versailles. Passes are valid for one, three, or five consecutive days and can be bought at museum ticket offices, tourist offices, and main métro stations. You'll make a saving if you visit just two museums per day (even fewer for the 5-day pass). When buying your ticket make sure you get the free booklet detailing all the museums you can visit with your pass.

Paris is home to countless museums. These are some of the most important:

Musée du Louvre (The Louvre), the vast palace with huge collections, especially ancient Egyptian, Greek, and Roman art, and European painting up to 1848. Open 9am-6pm (Napoleon Hall 10pm); closed Tuesday; free admission on the first Sunday in the month. Métro: Palais-Royal-Musée du Louvre. (See page 67)

Musée d'Orsay, the brilliantly converted former railway station is the home of a breathtaking collection of European art, especially French, from 1848 to 1914. Open 9am-6pm (summer and Sunday in winter); 10am-6pm (winter); Thursdays to 9:45pm; closed Monday. Métro: Solférino (RER Musée d'Orsay). (See page 69)

Centre Georges Pompidou (Musée National d'Art Moderne), an extraordinary building benefiting a collection featuring 20th-century art in all its eccentric variety. Open noon-10pm; weekends and public holidays 10am-10pm; closed Tuesday and 1 May. Most of the museum is closed until 2000. Métro: Rambuteau, Hôtel-de-Ville, Châtelet. (See page 70)

Musée d'Art Moderne de la Ville de Paris, a 20th-century collection to rival the Pompidou Centre's, and fewer crowds. It is especially strong on Braque, Matisse, Utrillo, Dufy, Delauney, and Chagall. The monumental 1937 Palais de Tokio is an exhibit in its own right. Open 10am-5:45pm; closed Monday. Métro: Iéna, Alma-Marceau.

Musée de l'Homme, in the 1937 Palais de Chaillot, huge collections of fossils, prehistoric artefacts, world-wide ethnology. Open 9:45am-5:15pm; closed Tuesday. Métro: Trocadéro.

Musée National du Moyen Age (Musée de Cluny), art of the Middle Ages, in the broadest sense, from first-century Roman to around 1500, housed in an old abbey, and the massive remains of the Roman baths. Open 9:15am-5:45pm; closed Tuesday. Métro: Saint-Michel, Cluny, Maubert-Mutualité. (See page 72)

Musée de l'Orangerie, a pavilion in the corner of the Tuileries gardens, with Monet murals and the superb Walther-Guillaume Collection of Impressionist and post-Impressionist art. Open 9:45am-5:15pm; closed Tuesday. Métro: Concorde. (See page 71)

Musée Rodin, a fine 18th-century mansion and its garden, with the definitive collection of works by the great sculptor. Open 10am-5:45pm (5pm, October-March); closed Monday. Métro: Varenne.

Musée Picasso, (See page 71) the artist's collection of his own work, as well as many pictures by his friends and contemporaries, in a fine old house and garden in the Marais. Open 9:30am-6pm (5:30pm, winter); closed Tuesday. Métro: Chemin Vert, Saint-Paul. (See page 71)

Palais de la Découverte, mainly intended for a young audience, with plenty of hands-on exhibits about science and exploration, as well as a planetarium. Open 9:30am-6pm; Sunday 10am-7pm; closed Monday. Métro: Champs-Elysées-Clémenceau, Franklin-Roosevelt.

Musée Carnavalet (Musée de l'Histoire de Paris), documents, engravings, and paintings bring Paris's history to life. In an outstanding exhibit devoted to the Revolution, a letter from Robespierre is dramatically stained with the author's blood: he was arrested and wounded while signing it. Open 10am-5:40pm; closed Monday. Métro: Saint-Paul, Chemin Vert, Bastille. (See page 50)

Cité des Sciences et de l'Industrie (La Villette), in a vast park on the north-eastern outskirts, exhibitions with plenty of audio-visual and interactive displays, 3D and 360° films, and much more, designed to educate and entertain. Open 10am-6pm; Sunday 7pm; closed Monday. Métro: Porte de la Villette. (See page 72) away, towering above the old town and the surrounding plain. Its medieval stained glass, including three fine rose windows, is of unrivalled complexity and stunning beauty. Climb to the roof for the extraordinary view of the stonework and flying buttresses.

Situated 88 km (55 miles) southwest of Paris by the A11 or N10, or by train from Gare Montparnasse. A large number of companies run bus tours from Paris. Open 7:00 A.M.–7:30 P.M. daily (7:30 A.M. – 7:00 P.M. October – March). The crypt and tower, and sometimes the cathedral itself, may be closed at lunch time.

FONTAINEBLEAU — Many visitors find the château more appealing and certainly less daunting than Versailles. It was a royal palace for much longer, with certain additions made over seven centuries, notably by François I in the 16th century. The adjoining town is charming and the surrounding forest, cool and shaded even in the hottest summer, is perfect for gentle walks, cycle rides, and picnics.

Situated 64 km (40 miles) southeast of Paris by the A6 or by train from Gare de Lyon and then bus to the château. Bus tours from Paris are available. Open 9:30 A.M. – 12:30 P.M., 2:00 –5:00 P.M. Closed Tuesday.

GIVERNY — These magnificent floral and water gardens were laid out by Claude Monet, who lived in Giverny from 1883 to 1926. He painted them many times, especially the waterlilies.

Situated 85 km (53 miles) northwest of Paris by the A13, D181, and D5, or by train from Gare St-Lazare to Vernon. A shuttle bus brings you from the station to Giverny, about 10 miles away. The house is open April – October, 10:00 A.M. – noon, 2:00 – 6:00 P.M. The gardens are open all year, 10:00 A.M. – 6:00 P.M. Closed Monday. The best time to go is in the morning (to beat the crowds) during the springtime (for the most impressive flower displays).

MALMAISON — Set in lovely grounds, the château used to be the home of Napoleon's wife, the Empress Josephine, who continued to live here after their divorce. Many of her possessions are on display in the various private and state apartments open to visitors.

Located 6 km (4 miles) west of Paris. Métro: Grande Arche de La Défense, then bus 258, or RER to rueil-Malmaison, and then walk. Open 10:30 A.M. – noon, 1:30 – 5:30 P.M. (4:30 P.M. in winter). Closed Tuesday.

VAUX-LE-VICOMTE — A splendid 17th-century château and gardens designed by Le Vau, Le Nôtre, and Le Brun for Louis XIV's finance minister, Fouquet. No sooner was the magnificent project completed than the king had its owner arrested for embezzlement and jailed for life.

Fontainebleau was a favourite residence for many French rulers, from François I to Napoleon.

Situated 56 km (35 miles) southeast of Paris on the N5, or by train from Gare de Lyon to Melun, and then taxi. Open daily 10:00 A.M. – 6:00 P.M. (11:00 A.M. – 5:00 P.M. November – March). Closed in January.

VERSAILLES — Louis XIV, the "Sun King," was quite simply a megalomaniac, but he also had extraordinary vision. He was wary of Paris and its rabble (all too easily roused) and rising aristocracy (ever-demanding and arrogant). What better way to keep potential trouble-makers under his thumb than to coop them up at Versailles, and let them squabble for rights and privileges as futile as attending His Majesty's awakening?

Versailles is as extravagant, formidable, and vainglorious as the man himself. Louis XIII had hoped to turn his favourite hunting ground into a modest retirement home, but his son and heir made it the centre of a universe, proclaiming his own grandeur in an edifice of brick, marble, gilt, and crystal.

The enormous courtyard of Versailles contains a statue of its creator, Louis XIV, the "Sun King."

A visit to the château takes most or all of a day, entails a lot of walking, and shouldn't be inflicted on young children. Bus tours leave from the Tuileries gardens on the rue de Rivoli side but you may prefer to do things in your own time. Make an early start, travel by RER (see page 123), and you can fit in a morning tour of part of the palace; stroll through the gardens; have lunch beside the Grand Canal (a packed lunch allows you to avoid Versailles' tourist traps); take tea in the grounds of the Petit Trianon; and finally wander back across the palace gardens for a last view of the château at sunset.

The central section of the building (where the royal family lived) was conceived by Louis Le Vau, Jules Hardouin-Mansart, and landscape designer André Le Nôtre in 1661. It was completed 21 years later. Le Vau also designed the marble courtyard, decorated with 84 marble busts.

Highlights of the vast interior include the **Royal Chapel**, a gem of high Baroque; the **State Apartments** in which Louis XIV used to entertain; the Salon de Diane, where he would try his hand at billiards; the glittering **Hall of Mirrors** (*Galerie des Glaces*), 73 metres (240 feet) long and built to catch the setting sun in 17 tall, arched panels of mirrors. Adjoining it is the King's bedroom, where Louis died of gangrene of the leg in 1715. In the Queen's bedroom, 19 royal children were born, the births often attended by members of the public, as was the custom. Several parts of the château, including Louis XV's superb **Royal Opera**, have to be visited on separate guided tours.

The most impressive façade faces west, to the gardens; the pretty fountains begin to play at 3:30 P.M. on three Sundays a month, from May to September. You should also look at the **Grand Trianon**, the small palace that Louis XIV used on occasions when he wanted to get away from the château, the **Petit Trianon** favoured by Louis XV, and the marvellous

Hameau (little village) and miniature farm where Marie-Antoinette, queen of Louis XVI, famously played at the simple life. They're some way from the château and each other; a little train runs a shuttle service, at a price.

Versailles is situated 24 km (15 miles) southwest of Paris, by road (N10); or by train from Gare St-Lazare to Versailles; or by RER (line C5) to Versailles-Rive Gauche; or by métro to Pont de Sèvres, then bus 171. The château is open 9:00 A.M. – 6:30 P.M. (winter 5:30 P.M.); the Grand and Petit Trianon 10:00 A.M. – 6:30 P.M. (10 A.M. – 12:30 P.M. and 2:00 – 5:30 P.M. Tuesday – Friday, 10:00 A.M. – 5:30 P.M. Saturday and Sunday in winter); the gardens 7:00 A.M. – sunset. Closed Monday.

DISNEYLAND PARIS — Much more than a theme park, Disney's ambitious recreation complex also encompasses hotels, camping facilities, restaurants, a convention centre, a championship golf course, tennis courts, and several swimming pools.

In the theme park itself, Main Street USA, recapturing the traditions of small-town America at the turn of the century, leads to four other "lands" — Frontierland, Adventureland, Fantasyland, and Discoveryland. Each themed section has a variety of fun experiences on offer. Hosts Mickey and Minnie Mouse, Goofy, Donald Duck, and Pluto wander around in their familiar costumes, posing with visitors but never speaking. Every day at 3:00 P.M. there's a spectacular all-singing, all-dancing parade including floats inspired by the famous Disney movies. For further information about day-to-day happenings in Disneyland Paris, telephone 64 74 30 00.

Situated 32 km (20 miles) east of Paris, close by Marne-la-Vallée. A motorway (*autoroute*) gives access from the city and the airports, Charles-de-Gaulle and Orly. Speedy commuter trains (RER line A) from the capital and even faster long-distance trains (TGV) serve Marne-la-Vallée/Chessy station near the entrance.

WHAT TO DO

Paris shops, ranging from high-fashion salons and small specialist shops to flea markets, are among the best in the world. You'll probably get enough exercise from all the walking you'll be doing, but plenty of facilities exist for both fitness fanatics and sports spectating. Dining (see page 138) is serious business in Paris, and street life the best free show. In terms of organized entertainment, Paris is still in love with the movies, and the music scene is especially diverse.

SHOPPING

The majority of shops and department stores are open from 9:00 A.M. to 7:00 P.M., Tuesday to Saturday. Some shops close at lunch-time from noon till 2:00 P.M. and many are closed on Monday mornings, if not all day Monday. The first to open their doors are usually the bakeries (*boulangerie*), and there's always a small grocer (*épicerie*) or mini-supermarket in which you can shop till 9:00 or 10:00 P.M., or even midnight. The Marais is the only district where shops open on Sunday. The drugstore at the top of the Champs-Elysées is open until 2:00 A.M. every night for snacks, takeaways, books, assorted gifts, and essentials.

The streets and lanes of Paris are a paradise for anyone who enjoys shopping.

In Galeries Lafayette, don't miss the gorgeous Art-Nouveau glass dome, dating from 1900.

Department Stores. The old **Galeries Lafayette** on boulevard Haussmann stocks a wide range of clothes at all price levels. Fashion shows are held at 11:00 A.M. on Wednesdays and also Fridays in summer. The china department is huge, and the cosmetics, sportswear, and luggage sections excellent. **Au Printemps**, just next door, has the biggest selection of shoes and is famous for its perfumes, toys, and innovative household goods. Fashion shows are at 10:00 A.M. on Tuesdays as well as Fridays in summer.

FNAC belongs to the newer, younger generation of department stores. Branches at l'Etoile, Montparnasse, and the Forum des Halles, as well as La Défense, have selections of books, discount CDs and cassettes, electronics, and sports goods. **Virgin Megastore**, on the Champs-Elysées, has an even bigger stock of CDs.

Marks & Spencers and **C&A** have Paris branches, but more typically French are **Au Bon Marché** at Sèvres-Babylone, which has an excellent men's department and a fabulous lingerie section. At **La Samaritaine** opposite Pont-Neuf (at 75 rue de Rivoli), you'll find everything from home furnishings to pets, and a splendid view of the city from its 10th-floor terrace.

The large modern **shopping malls** include the Forum des Halles, Centre Maine-Montparnasse, and the Palais des Congrès at Porte Maillot.

Fashion and Accessories. Almost synonymous with chic style, Paris remains paramount in the fashion stakes, despite hot competition. Most of the *couture* houses are concentrated on the Right Bank close by the rue du Faubourg-Saint-Honoré (just "Le Faubourg" to regular shoppers) and classier avenue Montaigne where designers Christian Lacroix, Chanel, Calvin Klein, Hermès, Christian Dior, Yves Saint Laurent, and Gianni Versace, to name a few, have shops. From here and over to Les Halles and place des Victoires, the *haute couture* houses and ready-to-wear (*prêt-à-porter*) boutiques have spread to the Left Bank around Saint-Germain-des-Prés.

Stores such as Dorothée-Bis, Benetton, and the less expensive but lower quality Tati are found throughout the capital; there's a branch at Barbès-Rochechouart, but be prepared to jostle. Children's clothes are fun and stylish too, though you may balk at the prices. Try chains such as Jacadi or Tartine et Chocolat.

VAT Exemption

Visitors from outside the European Union can claim exemption from sales taxes (TVA) if they spend more than 2,000F on purchases from a single shop; the sum can be made up of various items. EU residents do not qualify. Department stores and luxury goods shops are used to dealing with foreign visitors. Staff will provide a form, *bordereau de vente* (export sales invoice); you then have it stamped by customs as you leave France or the EU and mail it back to the store to reclaim the tax. The shop eventually sends you a refund in French francs. You'll generally get reimbursed faster if you pay by credit card.

Nostalgia is the keynote in stalls by the Seine, selling prints, old magazines, and postcards.

Antiques. Antiques shops cluster around the Left Bank's 6th and 7th *arrondissements*. The Carré Rive Gauche, bounded by the quai Voltaire, the boulevard Saint-Germain, the rues du Bac, and des Saints-Pères, is something of a museum of ancient Egyptian, Chinese, pre-Columbian, African, and Polynesian art, as well as Louis XV, Second Empire, Art Nouveau, and Art Deco. Across the river, 250 dealers are concentrated in the Louvre des Antiquaires, by the place du Palais-Royal, closed Monday (and Sunday in July and August), and other antiques dealers are scattered around Les Halles.

Flea Markets (*Marchés aux Puces*). There's virtually no chance of picking up a treasure that has slipped through the hands of the experts, but it's fun to try. Many of the stands are run by professional dealers. The giant of the flea markets is Saint-Ouen at the Porte de Clignancourt, 75018, open from 6:00 A.M. to 7:00 P.M., Saturday, Sunday, and Monday. The market at Porte de Vanves, 75014, has a high proportion of junk (open Saturday and Sunday 6:00 A.M.-6:00 P.M.). You'll find bric-a-brac and old or second-hand clothes at Porte de Montreuil, 75020, open Saturday, Sunday, and Monday mornings. For inexpensive new clothes, pay a visit to the carreau du Temple, 75003, open every morning except Monday.

Books. Trade in old and new books flourishes on the Left Bank in or around the Latin Quarter, notably at the Odéon. Second-hand bookshops, commonly known as *bouquinistes*, line the quays of the Seine, especially between Pont Saint-Michel and Pont des Arts. It's worth rummaging through the mass of books, prints, postcards, and periodicals for occasional finds, though the asking prices may seem high.

If you're pining for English-language books try Brentano's at 37 avenue de l'Opéra, W.H. Smith at 248 rue de Rivoli, or the NQL (Nouveau Quartier Latin) at the head of boulevard Saint-Michel.

Food and Drink. Fine foods can make wonderful presents. Thanks to today's packaging methods, it's possible to transport goods that previously spoiled en route (but remember the bans on many food imports imposed by the United States and Australia, among others). Two famous luxury grocery shops, **Fauchon** and **Hédiard**, glare at each other across the place de la Madeleine. For **wines**, the Nicolas chain has a wide range at its 150 Paris branches. A bigger selection is at Legrand, on rue de la Banque. Spirits (liquor) and liqueurs may be less expensive at the duty-free shops as you leave France, though note that the choice will be more limited.

> There are more than 300 different kinds of cheese in France.

Food Markets. Covered markets or street markets operate all over Paris, especially in the Left Bank. Try the photogenic rue de Buci in St-Germain-des-Prés, open every morning except Monday, or rue de la Convention in Montparnasse, near the Convention métro station, on Tuesday, Thursday, and Sunday mornings. The best one is on **rue Mouffetard**, behind the Panthéon, on Tuesday, Thursday, or Saturday morning.

The **flower** market in place Louis Lépine, near Notre-Dame on Ile de la Cité, opens from 8:00 A.M. to 7:30 P.M. daily. On

Sundays it switches to small pets, especially caged birds. The flower stalls in place de la Madeleine open daily except Monday.

SPORTS

There is *le jogging* in the big parks of the Bois de Boulogne and Bois de Vincennes, on the Champ du Mars under the Eiffel Tower, along the quays beside the Seine, in the Tuileries gardens and even by the Champs-Elysées. More of a

In spite of inroads made by the supermarkets, many Parisians still shop for food at market stalls.

challenge are the hilly Parc Montsouris (on the Left Bank) or Buttes-Chaumont (on the Right). An alternative is to hire a **bicycle** (see page 106). Ask at tourist offices for information on bike tours of the city and outlying areas such as Fontainebleau.

There are a number of public **tennis** courts in Paris, but it's first-come-first-serve, as at the Jardin du Luxembourg courts. Big hotels may arrange for their guests to play at one of the many tennis clubs.

Municipal pools are available for **swimming**. The most serious action takes place at the Olympic-size indoor pools in the Centre de Natation, at 34 boulevard Carnot, and the Forum des Halles shopping complex.

Among **spectator sports**, pride of place goes to **horse-racing**. The summer meetings at Longchamp (venue of the Prix de l'Arc de Triomphe), Auteuil, and Chantilly are as elegant as Britain's Ascot. The serious punter who wants to avoid the frills and Champagne can have a very good time at Vincennes and Enghien trotting races.

Rugby and **football** (soccer) can be seen at the modern stadium of Parc-des-Princes. **Tennis tournaments** usually take place at Roland-Garros. (Both of these venues are at the southern end of the Bois de Boulogne.) The Palais Omnisports de Paris-Bercy, near the Gare de Lyon, was designed for a variety of sports and stages everything from rock concerts to tango competitions, as well as cycle races and indoor windsurfing.

ENTERTAINMENT

To see what's on in Paris while you are there, buy one of the weekly guides, *Pariscope* or *L'Officiel des Spectacles*, with comprehensive listings of all kinds of entertainment.

The cinema is a great national passion, with 300 different **films** showing every week in the capital. For undubbed versions with French subtitles, look out for the letters VO (*version originale*) in the listings or posters. Cinemas on the Champs-Elysées and in the Forum des Halles tend to show movies in VO.

Keeping up with the latest in **discos** and **clubs** can be a full-time job for professional night-owls: there's no point in turning up before midnight. Many are nominally private, which means you only get in if the doormen like the way you look and think you're going to spend. Some expensive, exclusive examples hide out around the Champs-Elysées, such as Régine's in the rue de Ponthieu. Louder, less expensive, younger, and

Trotting races are a favourite Parisian spectator sport — and an excuse for a bet.

weirder places come and go around Bastille and Oberkampf. There's still some life in Saint-Germain-des-Prés and the Latin Quarter, especially in university term time — making local friends is the best way to find it.

Pop and rock concerts are held at the spectacular Zénith in the Parc de la Villette (métro: Porte de Pantin) and also at Parc-des-Princes (métro: Porte de St-Cloud) and the Palais Omnisport de Bercy (métro: Bercy). The basement *billeterie* at Virgin Megastore on the Champs-Elysées is the place to find out what groups are in town.

The French take their **jazz** seriously, and Paris has many jazz clubs. Hot Brass (La Villette) and The New Morning (rue des Petites-Ecuries) attracts the big American and European musicians, while Le Dunois (rue Dunois) is an intimate place, cultivating more avant-garde music. The Lionel Hampton club at the Méridien Etoile (Porte Maillot) has a full programme of guest performers. The old-established Caveau de la Huchette (rue de la Huchette in St-Germain-des-Prés) opens every night at 9:30 P.M. for listening and dancing to a small combo or big band swing or bebop. Entrance prices of around 60-120F may include your first drink; extra drinks cost 30-60F.

In the realm of **classical music**, Paris has come back into its own, with many fine concerts at Théâtre des Champs-Elysées, the National Opera at the modern Opéra-Bastille, and the National Ballet at the Opéra-Garnier. In all cases, some seats are reasonably priced, though they tend to go quickly. Look out for free concerts in churches.

Modern **dance** is enjoying a revival, with a new wave of small, imaginative companies beginning modestly enough at the Café de la Danse (passage Louis-Philippe) and Théâtre Garnier before reaching the heights of the Théâtre de la Bastille.

With some command of the French language, **theatre** lovers can enjoy the classics by Molière, Racine, or

Corneille at the Comédie Française (rue de Richelieu).

The naughty image of Paris has a long history and isn't dead yet. The Folies Bergères (rue Richer), which launched the careers of Josephine Baker, Mistinguett, and Maurice Chevalier, and the Lido on the Champs-Elysées are both classic survivors. The most famous modern-day floor show, chic as well as erotic and brilliantly choreographed, is at the Crazy Horse Saloon (avenue George V). Toulouse-Lautrec painted the showgirls of the Moulin Rouge (place Blanche) a century ago, and it still puts on a boisterous floor show in the old tradition, though mainly for the busloads of tourists nowadays. The rest of Pigalle plumbs the lower depths with a certain glee that continues to fascinate visitors.

PARIS FOR CHILDREN

From dawn to dusk, a lot of the activities that interest adults are fortunately likely to appeal to children as well. Boat trips (see page 24) especially are good fun for everyone. The **Jardin d'Acclimatation** in the Bois de Boulogne (see page 65) is a special children's park, complete with a small zoo, pony rides, puppet shows and other attractions (open daily,

Two great institutions face place de l'Opéra: the Café de la Paix and Opéra-Garnier.

10:00 A.M.-6:00 P.M.). The capital's main zoo, open daily, 9:00 A.M.-5:30 P.M. (6:00 P.M. during summer), is located in the Bois de Vincennes (métro: Porte Dorée).

Small children are bound to enjoy the merry-go-round and pony rides in the **Jardin du Luxembourg**, where they can also watch the toy boats capsize in the fountain. For the scientifically minded, there's a great deal to learn painlessly at the Cité des Sciences et de l'Industrie at **La Villette** (see page 72). The **Palais de la Découverte** (see page 75) makes use of a similar hands-on approach.

Some 30 km (20 miles) outside Paris at Marne-la-Vallée, the **Disneyland Paris** resort could keep kids happy for several days (see page 80). Fans of the Astérix comics about ancient Gauls and Romans will enjoy the theme park, **Parc Astérix**, near *Autoroute* A1 between Roissy and Senlisi, open from April to October; tel. 03 44 62 34 34. **France Miniature** is a 5 hectare (7½ acre) relief map of France including model villages, châteaux, and monuments to a scale of 1:30 (RER train to St-Quentin-en-Yvelines, then bus; open daily, 15 March–15 November).

There's plenty of fun on offer besides the obvious attractions for children in Paris.

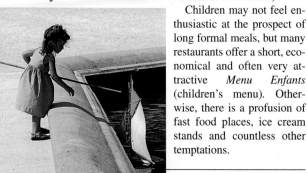

Children may not feel enthusiastic at the prospect of long formal meals, but many restaurants offer a short, economical and often very attractive *Menu Enfants* (children's menu). Otherwise, there is a profusion of fast food places, ice cream stands and countless other temptations.

EATING OUT

Dining out is one of the greatest pleasures of Paris. Indeed, for some visitors it's the main objective of their visit. If you have a particular restaurant in mind it's as well to reserve (far ahead for the famous names). Otherwise, finding a place to eat is part of the enjoyment. In areas where restaurants are concentrated, you can take a look at a selection, sharpening your appetite while you stroll around. Restaurants are obliged to display priced menus outside, so you can compare them, including the day's specials *(plats du jour).* One of the best recommendations is the sight of a crowd inside, especially if it's local people (conversely, note that such places may be empty early in the evening). If there's too long a wait for a table, make a reservation for some other day. (See RECOMMENDED RESTAURANTS, page 138.)

> You'd be hard pressed to find all-you-can-eat restaurants. Food is a matter of quality, and quantity has nothing to do with it.

WHERE TO LOOK

No part of Paris is lacking in places to eat, but some areas offer an especially wide range.

On the Left Bank, try between boulevard Saint-Germain and Pont-Neuf, around rue Saint-Séverin, in the rue Mouffetard and its extension, rue Descartes, and in the area behind Gare Montparnasse.

On the Right Bank, start by looking around Les Halles and the Centre Pompidou, place de la Bastille and the Marais — including the Jewish quarter. Farther to the west, look between place de l'Opéra and boulevard Haussmann, to the north of Champs-Elysées and also near avenue Wagram, north of place des Ternes.

From mid-July to the end of August, many restaurant owners close up and go off on holiday, reducing the choice.

Menus

A boon to everyone on a budget is the fixed price *table d'hôte* or *menu fixe*, *prix fixe*, or just *menu* (remember, the French word for menu is not *menu* but *carte*). The word *formule* similarly means an all-inclusive special deal. There's frequently the option of starter + main course *or* main course + dessert (or cheese). A drink may be included in the price — either a small carafe of wine, a beer, soft drink, or mineral water. In this case you may see the letters b.c. (*boisson comprise*) or v.c. (*vin compris*).

Don't even try to resist the miniature masterpieces created by the Paris pastry chefs.

Competition has done wonders in recent years and, in general, you get what you pay for, so a 69F *formule* will be simple and the portions probably quite small. If you are on a tight budget, watch out for high-priced extras — apéritifs or coffee — which can add up to as much again as the basic meal. Never order anything without knowing the price.

Tax and service charge are included, signified by t.s.c., s.t.c., or s.c. (*service compris*) at the foot of the menu. If you pay by credit card, the "extras" line and the total may be left open for you to write in a tip. There is no obligation to do so, as tipping is not common practice in France. In theory, restaurants must provide a designated non-smoking area, but avoiding smokers is a difficult feat in Paris.

The Options

At traditional, rather formal **restaurants**, with their own style and speciality dishes, you will be expected to reserve a table, dress up to a degree, and spend most of an evening. But there are many other possibilities (although the boundaries between them are blurred). A *bistro* is likely to be small, informal, and family-run,

Sidewalk eating is a good way to enjoy the ambience and flavour of Paris.

and might have lace curtains, tiled floors, wood panelling, and red check tablecloths. A modern version may go in for vivid colours, high-tech lighting, and strange furniture. Wine comes by the carafe, plus a few bottles, perhaps listed on the back of the single-page menu. A *bistro à vin* (wine bar) makes more of its wines and less of its food, which may be bread and cheese, sausages, quiches. A **pub** in Paris can be facsimile British or Irish, or the local version, usually with a range of beers and hot meals too. Beer comes bottled or draft (*pression*), which costs less. A *demi* is 50cl, less than a pint.

A **brasserie** combines the functions of bar, café, and restaurant and keeps long hours: some never close at all. They are simply furnished, brightly lit, and can be huge. You can order anything from a drink to a snack or full dinner. Alsatian cuisine is common.

A **café** sells more than just coffee: you can have a beer, apéritif, soft drink, or snack, even a hot dish of the day (*plat du jour*). You pay more sitting at a table than at the stand-up counter — a cup of coffee could cost twice as much, but you can linger over it for hours. Coffee, incidentally, is *un express*, a small black coffee, unless you specify otherwise (*au lait* is with hot milk).

Many of the older generation in Paris like to meet at a **salon de thé**, for a pastry or slice of fruit tart and a cup of tea in the afternoon. Some salons will serve a light lunch too.

Despite this broad choice of eating places, **vegetarians** have a tough time. In practice, it's easy to avoid meat, with plenty of salads, fish, cheese, and egg-based dishes, and

---

Economy Measures

- Find a tasty-sounding *formule* or *menu* and avoid any extras.
- Remember, restaurants cost less at lunch-time and might come within your budget; consider making lunch your main meal.
- Try the ethnic restaurants, and unfashionable parts of Paris — like the east and northeast.
- Buy sandwiches, filled lengths of French bread, from bakeries and grocery stores — prices get inflated at sandwich bars near to tourist sights. Better still, pick up ingredients for a picnic at one of the mini-supermarkets, and look for a bench in a park or beside the Seine.
- Fast food is all over the city, including the usual international names. A big step up in quality but still budget-priced are local chains such as Hippopotamus and Bistro Romain.

restaurant chains as well as some chefs are starting to list vegetarian choices.

Ethnic Variations

Parisians have taken to ethnic restaurants in a big way, and nowadays you can find almost as many variations as nations at the UN. Chinese restaurants were among the first, and many of them are now luxurious establishments around the Champs-Elysées area and Les Halles. Vietnamese, Laotian, and Cambodian food has caught on, with dozens of places to be found in the Latin Quarter and the 13th *arrondissement*, behind the place d'Italie, home to numerous immigrants from Southeast Asia. Their cuisine features distinctive touches of mint, coriander, lemon-grass (*citronelle*), and ginger, and a great variety of seafood. Thai restaurants have multiplied in Paris, as they have in almost every western capital. More and more Japanese restaurants also appear each year, with plenty of tourists from Japan to encourage a certain degree of authenticity.

Neighbourhood cafés can serve as bar, club, snack bar, and centre for gossip — all in one.

Greek, Turkish, and Lebanese restaurants are scattered along the Left Bank, notably in the Latin Quarter. The shabby north-eastern suburb of Belleville, home to a sizeable Algerian and Moroccan community, has the most authentic North African cooking. Italian restaurants may be found virtually everywhere. Indian food is also making

great headway, going beyond simple curries and Tandoori to the wonderful subtleties of the Mughal and Kashmiri cuisines.

Wines

French wine lists rarely mention anything that isn't French. The great names of Bordeaux and Burgundy, and of course Champagne, are still the ones the rest of the world wants to beat, but there's a host of other regional wines too, much more reasonably priced.

> **Wine is not consumed with salads or other dishes with vinegar preparations. Combining the two could result in a strange taste.**

Usually only the top-flight restaurants have wine waiters (*sommeliers*) who know much about the subject. They'll be happy if you seek their help, and probably unruffled if you don't. Elsewhere, the regular waiter or waitress will take your wine order. Mark-ups are generally high (three to four times that of wine store prices), so unless you see a known favourite, it's just as well to go for a carafe (*pichet*) of the house wine (*vin de la maison*). Most French people will be doing the same. In summer, don't be surprised if the red wine comes chilled (*frais*). It's the custom, and an easy one to get used to.

You can eat simply and well, without spending a fortune — try the set menu at a brasserie.

Riches of the Regions

Every part of France proclaims the superiority of its cooking. Paris, with no distinctive cuisine of its own, is a showcase for them all.

Burgundy produces a great beef stew, *bœuf bourguignon*, beef simmered in red wine with mushrooms, small white onions, and a little bacon. Its Bresse poultry is considered France's finest, and the Charolais beef provides the most tender steaks.

Lyon is renowned for its pork, game, vegetables, and fruit. Onion soup (*soupe à l'oignon*) is a local invention; and *à la lyonnaise* generally means sautéed with onions. Dishes include (for starters): *cœurs d'artichaut* (artichoke hearts), or *gratin de queues d'écrevisses* (baked crayfish tails).

Alsace is next to Germany, and does some similar dishes — smoked pork, dumplings, and *choucroute* (sauerkraut, or pickled cabbage) — but, the French would argue, better!

Brittany is celebrated for its shellfish, served unadorned on a bed of crushed ice and seaweed, as a *plateau de fruits de mer*. It will often include raw oysters, and steamed mussels, clams, scallops, prawns, and whelks.

Normandy is famous for its dairy farms. Cream and butter are staples of the cuisine, while the local apples (*reinettes*) turn up with flambéed partridge (*perdreau flambé aux reinettes*) and in *poulet au Calvados* (chicken with apple-brandy sauce). Besides Camembert cheese, sample the stronger Livarot or Pont-l'Evêque.

Bordeaux gave its name to *bordelaise* sauce, made with white or red wine, shallots, and beef marrow, served variously with entrecôte steaks, cèpe mushrooms, or lamprey eels (*lamproies*).

Provence makes the most of its garlic, olives, tomatoes, and the country's most fragrant herbs. Spicy *tapenade*, an olive and anchovy paste, is delicious on toast. *Daube de bœuf* is beef stew with tomatoes and olives. The celebrated *bouillabaisse* soup should contain half a dozen or more sorts of fish and shellfish — a meal in itself.

The southwestern regions of Gascony and Périgord are famous for foie gras (goose liver), and for confit d'oie and confit de canard, rich goose and duck preserves, traditionally kept for winter feasting.

To Help You Order . . .

Do you have a table?	**Avez-vous une table?**
I would like (a/an/some) ...	**J'aimerais ...**
The bill, please	**L'addition** (or **la note**)
	s'il vous plait

beer	**une bière**	mineral water	**de l'eau minérale**
butter	**du beurre**		
bread	**du pain**	sparkling/	**gazeuse/**
cheese	**du fromage**	still	**plat**
chips (fries)	**des frites**	pepper	**du poivre**
coffee	**un café**	salad	**une salade**
dessert	**un dessert**	salt	**du sel**
fish	**du poisson**	seafood	**fruits de mer**
glass	**un verre**	soup	**de la soupe**
meat	**de la viande**	sugar	**du sucre**
menu	**la carte**	tea	**du thé**
milk	**du lait**	wine	**du vin...**

Savoury and sweet Arabic specialities are ideal for a picnic break between sightseeing.

. . . and Read the Menu

agneau	lamb	**jambon**	ham
asperges	asparagus	**langouste**	rock lobster
bar	sea bass	**lapin**	rabbit
boeuf	beef	**moules**	mussels
caille	quail	**nouilles**	noodles
canard	duck	**oignons**	onions
caneton	duckling	**petits pois**	peas
cerises	cherries	**pintade**	guinea fowl
champignons	mushrooms	**poire**	pear
charcuterie	cold cooked meats/sausage	**poireaux**	leeks
chou	cabbage	**pomme**	apple
choufleur	cauliflower	**pomme de terre**	potato
crevettes roses/grises	prawns/shrimps	**porc**	pork
crudités	raw vegetables	**poulet**	chicken
daurade	sea bream	**raisins**	grapes
échalotes	shallots	**ris de veau**	calf's sweet breads
épinards	spinach		
farci	stuffed	**riz**	rice
foie	liver	**rognon**	kidney
fraises	strawberries	**rouget**	red mullet
framboises	raspberries	**saucisse**	sausage
haricots verts	green beans	**saumon**	salmon
homard	lobster	**thon**	tuna
huitres	oysters	**truite**	trout
		veau	veal

So how would you like your steak?

very rare	**bleu**	medium	**à point**
rare	**saignant**	well done	**bien cuit**
medium-rare	**rose**		

INDEX

HANDY TRAVEL TIPS

An A–Z Summary of Practical Information

A

ACCOMMODATION *(see also* RECOMMENDED HOTELS *starting on page 130,* YOUTH HOSTELS *on page 128, and* CAMPING *on page 107)*

Paris has hotels to suit every taste and budget. The city is a popular destination all year round, so booking in advance in any season is recommended. See page 106 for information about making reservations at the airport. During big commercial fairs rooms are hard to find.

Hotels are officially classified into five categories, from one to five stars, determined by comfort and amenities; a complete booklet is available from the Paris Tourist Information Office (see page 121). Rates naturally depend on the hotel's amenities and location, and are posted visibly at reception desks.

Relatively few hotels have air-conditioning, but it rarely gets so hot that you'd miss it. Still, you might want to have the windows open in summer, so ask for a room that doesn't face a noisy street.

For a long stay you might consider renting. Travel sections of national newspapers carry advertisements and, on the spot, *Le Figaro,* the *International Herald Tribune,* and *France – U.S.A. Contacts* (available at expat hangouts and embassies) list accommodations for rent.

Do you have a single/double room for tonight?	**Avez-vous une chambre pour une/deux personnes pour cette nuit?**
What's the rate per night?	**Quel est le prix pour une nuit?**

AIRPORTS *(aéroport)*

Paris has two main airports. Roissy-Charles-de-Gaulle is about 25 km (15 miles) northeast of the city and has two terminals, CDG 1 for most international flights; CDG 2 mainly for Air France flights. Orly (for most domestic and many European flights) is about 15 km (9 miles) to the south, with two buildings, Orly-Sud and Orly-Ouest. Both airports have exchange facilities, good restaurants, snack-bars, post offices, and duty-free shops.

Paris

Regular **buses** link the two main airports with Paris and each other, and run frequently from about 6am to 11pm. The city terminals (*aérogare*) for Charles-de-Gaulle airport are at Porte Maillot, near l'Etoile, and at Opéra (rue Scribe); you can also board the bus at the Arc de Triomphe (avenue Carnot). *Roissybus* from Opéra takes about 45 minutes. Orly is served by buses to the Invalides city terminal (40 minutes journey) and by the *Orlybus* (every 15 minutes to/from Denfert-Rochereau RER station, taking about 30 minutes).

Taxis are plentiful, but more expensive from the airport (see page 124).

RER trains run every 15 minutes from about 5:30am to 11:30pm between Charles-de-Gaulle airport and Gare du Nord; the trip takes 35-40 minutes. Orly is served by *Orlyval* trains which connect with RER line B (opposite platform) to central Paris; alternatively, use RER Line C which runs to the Gare d'Austerlitz, Saint-Michel, and Musée d'Orsay stations: journey time is about 35 minutes.

Hotel reservations can be made in the airport arrival halls. At CDG 1 go to Porte 36, where a desk is open from 7:30am to 11pm. (A deposit of 12% is required, which will be deducted from the bill.) Alternatively, the electronic notice board next to the desk enables you to contact (free of charge) a wide range of hotels throughout the city. CDG 2 has similar amenities. For further general information, call (01) 48 62 22 80 (Charles-de-Gaulle) or (01) 49 75 15 15 (Orly). Most staff speak English.

B

BICYCLE HIRE (RENTAL) *(location de bicyclettes)*

You can hire bikes by the day or week, for example at: Paris-Vélo, 2 rue du Fer à Moulin, 75005; tel. 06 09 21 14 59, and Mountain Bike Trip, 6 place Etienne Pernet, 75015; tel. (01) 48 42 57 87.

These and other companies also run guided tours by bicycle: tourist information offices can supply a longer list. In the Bois de Boulogne, old-fashioned bikes are available by the hour near the Jardin d'Acclimatation (see page 65). You'll be asked for an identity document or a large deposit.

C

CAMPING

The only site reasonably close to the centre of Paris is in the Bois de Boulogne, beside the Seine. It gets crowded in summer. A number of other sites are in striking distance, at Champigny-sur-Marne, Torcy, and St-Quentin-en-Yvelines, all on the RER suburban train network.

CAR HIRE (RENTAL) *(location de voitures)*

Local firms may offer lower prices than international companies, but the latter will often let you return the car at any branch in the country at no extra cost. Ask about seasonal and other special deals.

To hire a car, you must show your driving licence (held for at least a year) and sometimes passport. You also need a major credit card, or a large deposit will be required. The minimum age for hiring cars ranges from 20 to 23, and a maximum of 65 is imposed by some companies. Third-party insurance is compulsory, but full cover is recommended.

Yellow Pages *(Pages Jaunes)* list the companies, under *Location de voitures*.

I'd like to hire a car now/tomorrow.	**Je voudrais louer une voiture tout de suite/demain.**
for one day/a week	**pour une journée/une semaine**

CLIMATE and CLOTHING

Paris enjoys a mild continental climate. Extremes of heat or cold are rare, although in July and August daytime temperatures sometimes exceed 30°C (86°F). In most respects, the best seasons for a visit are spring and autumn, though winter is perfectly bearable.

The chart below is for average monthly temperatures (daily high).

	J	F	M	A	M	J	J	A	S	O	N	D
temperature °C	8	7	10	16	17	23	25	26	21	17	12	8
temperature °F	46	45	50	61	63	73	77	79	70	63	54	46

Clothing. In common with most capitals, Paris is a lot less formal than it used to be but still dressier than London and New York. Most formal restaurants still expect men to wear a jacket and tie. In the heat of midsummer you will want to have light cotton clothing that you can wash and hang up to dry overnight. A raincoat is useful in winter, and an umbrella at any time. A pair of sturdy walking shoes is essential.

COMMUNICATIONS

Post Offices (*poste*). These display a stylized blue bird and the sign *La Poste*. They are usually open from 8am to 7pm Monday to Friday and 8am-noon on Saturday. The city's main post office at 52 rue du Louvre is open 24 hours a day, every day. The post office at 71, avenue des Champs-Elysées is open until 10pm on weekdays, and opens on Sundays and public holidays (10am-noon, 2-8pm).

As well as the usual mail services, you can make phone calls, buy *télécartes* (phone cards), and send faxes and telegrams.

Letters may be delivered within hours in the Paris district by sending them *postexpress* from the post office. Another quick system for delivering a message is the *message téléphoné*; tel. 36 55.

N.B. While you can theoretically buy stamps (*timbres poste*) at tobacconists (*tabacs*) or souvenir shops, the salespeople are disinclined to sell them unless you purchase something else. You can, however, buy phonecards there (see page 109).

Mail (*courrier*). If you don't know ahead of time where you'll be staying, you can have your mail addressed to you *poste restante* (general delivery) c/o Poste restante, 52 rue du Louvre, 75001 Paris (open always). You can collect it for a small fee on presentation of your passport. American Express, at 11 rue Scribe, 75009 Paris, performs the same service for card holders.

The **Minitel** computer terminal found in many French homes can be used for everything from making TGV train reservations to booking a theatre ticket, joining a dating service, or looking up someone's telephone number or address. Visitors can find one in most post offices: a phonecard is needed to operate it. You may need help from a French person at first although there's nothing very complicated about it. Instructions on screen are in French, but you may find a booklet in English at offices of France Télécom.

Telephones (*téléphone*). Long-distance and international calls can be made from any phone box, but if you need assistance, you can call from post offices or your hotel (you'll pay a supplement).

The system is efficient and simple, but Paris phone boxes only take **phonecards** (*télécartes*). You can buy cards of 50 or 120 units (48F or 96F respectively) at post offices or tobacconists. Don't get caught without one on a Sunday when few places selling them are open.

To make an **international** call, dial 00 followed by the country code, area code (omitting any initial zero) and number. For international inquiries, add 33 between 00 and the code of your chosen country, e.g. 00 33 44 (inquiries for the UK). For inquiries on US or Canadian numbers, dial 11 instead of 1 (i.e., 00 33 11).

The phone numbering system recently changed. Calling anywhere in France, be it next door or long distance, requires 10 digits. Paris numbers begin with 01, Normandy numbers begin with 02, Alsace numbers with 03, Provence numbers with 04, and Bordeaux numbers with 05. If all else fails, call the operator for help (12).

Faxes. Hotels can send them for you, though the charges can be high. Larger post offices offer fax services.

COMPLAINTS

If you have a complaint, make it on the spot, pleasantly and calmly, and to the correct person. At a hotel or restaurant, ask to speak to the manager (*directeur* or *maître d'hôtel*). In extreme cases only, a police station (*commissariat de police*) may help or, failing that, outside Paris, try the regional administration offices (the *préfecture* or *sous-préfecture*). Ask for the *service du tourisme*.

CRIME *(see also* LOST PROPERTY *on page 115)*

Keep items of value and any large amounts of money in hotel safe boxes. Beware of being crowded by street children whose aim is to get their fingers into your pockets or handbags. Never leave a car unlocked. Don't leave anything in view when parked, and if possible remove the radio. Avoid walking alone in dark streets and travelling late on the métro, though the risks are no greater than in most cities.

Any loss or theft should be reported as soon as possible to the nearest police station and to your embassy. A report will help with the insurance claim.

CUSTOMS (*douane*) and ENTRY FORMALITIES

Nationals of EU countries and Switzerland need only a valid passport or identity document to enter France. Nationals from Canada, New Zealand, and the USA require passports whilst Australian and South African nationals must obtain a visa. For the latest information on entry requirements, contact the French embassy in your country.

As France belongs to the European Union (EU), free exchange of non-duty-free goods for personal use is permitted between France and the UK and Eire. However, duty-free items are still subject to restrictions: again, check before you go.

For residents of non-EU countries, restrictions when going home are as follows:

Currency restrictions. There's no limit on the amount of local or foreign currencies or traveller's cheques that can be brought into France, but amounts in banknotes exceeding 50,000 French francs (or equivalent) should be declared if you intend to export them.

D

DRIVING

To take a car into France, you will need: a valid driving licence; car registration papers; insurance cover (the green insurance card is no longer obligatory but comprehensive cover is advisable); a red warning triangle and a set of spare bulbs are strongly recommended.

The minimum driving age is 18. Drivers and front- and back-seat passengers are required by law to wear seat belts. Children under 10 may not travel in the front (unless the car has no back seat). Driving on a foreign provisional licence is not permitted.

Driving regulations. As elsewhere on the continent, drive on the right, overtake (pass) on the left. At roundabouts (traffic circles), vehicles already in the roundabout have right of way. Otherwise, in built-up areas, give priority to vehicles coming from the right. In other areas, the more important of the two roads (indicated by a yellow diamond) has right of way. The use of car horns in built-up areas is allowed only as a warning. At night, lights should be used for this purpose (to let someone know you want to pass, for instance). Don't drink and drive: random breath tests are frequent and the alcohol limit is very low (corresponding to one **small** drink).

Speed limits. The limit is 50 km/h (31 mph) in built-up areas and 80 km/h (50 mph) on the *périphérique* ring road. Elsewhere it is 90 km/h (55 mph); 110 km/h (70 mph) on dual carriageways; 130 km/h (around 80 mph) on *autoroutes* (toll motorways). Note: when roads are wet, limits are reduced by 10 km/h (6 mph), and by 20 km/h (12 mph) on motorways. In fog, the limit is 50 km/h (31 mph). Police speed traps are common, and you can be fined heavily, on the spot, for offences.

Road conditions. Driving in Paris can be an exciting experience. Thanks to Haussmann's broad avenues and the Seine-side *voie express*, traffic generally sweeps through the capital at a tolerable speed — but you can't rely on it and horrendous jams can form. The ring road (*périphérique*) round Paris tends to get clogged at rush hours and summer weekends. Note that motorways (*autoroutes*) outside Paris are expensive. For advance information on traffic conditions, radio France-Inter's *Inter-Route* service operates 24 hours a day. Most of the time, English-speaking staff will be there to help you; tel. (01) 48 94 33 33.

Parking (*stationnement*). This is a nightmare (as in most capitals), which is why it's better to walk, use the métro, or take a bus. In the centre most street parking is metered and the spaces marked "*Payant.*" You buy a ticket at a nearby machine and display it inside the car. Never park in bus lanes, express lanes, or anywhere that isn't clearly permitted, or your car may be towed away to an obscure pound, only to be retrieved at great expense.

Breakdowns. It's wise to take out international breakdown insurance before leaving home. Always ask for an estimate before authorizing repairs, and expect to pay TVA (value-added tax) on top of the cost. Two companies which offer 24-hour breakdown service are Automobile Club Secours, tel. 08.00 05 05 24 (toll-free), and SOS Dépannage, tel. (01) 47 07 99 99.

Fuel and oil (*essence*; *huile*). Fuel is available as super (98 octane), normal (90 octane), lead-free (*sans plomb* — 98 or 95 octane) and diesel (gas-oil). Note that many garages are shut on Sundays. Avoid buying fuel on motorways: try to get to a supermarket to fill up — there can be as much as a 15% difference in price.

Road signs. Most signs are the standard pictographs used throughout Europe, but you may encounter these written signs as well:

Déviation	Diversion (detour)
Péage	Toll
Priorité à droite	Yield to traffic from right
Vous n'avez pas la priorité	Give way
Ralentir	Slow down
Serrez à droite/à gauche	Keep right/left
Sens unique	One way
Rappel	Restriction continues (a reminder)

driving licence	**permis de conduire**
car registration papers	**carte grise**
Fill the tank, please.	**Le plein, s'il vous plaît.**
My car has broken down.	**Ma voiture est en panne.**
There's been an accident.	**Il y a eu un accident.**

E

ELECTRIC CURRENT

You'll need an adaptor for most British and US plugs: French sockets have round holes. Supplies are 220 volt, and US equipment will need a transformer. Shaver outlets are generally dual voltage.

EMBASSIES and CONSULATES

For any major problem, such as loss of a passport or all your money, a serious accident or trouble with the police, contact your consulate or embassy.

Australia embassy and consulate: 4 rue Jean-Rey, 75015 Paris; tel. (01) 40 59 33 00; fax 01 40 59 35 38.

Canada embassy: 35 avenue Montaigne, 75008 Paris; tel. (01) 44 43 29 16; fax 01 44 43 29 93.

Republic of Ireland embassy: 12 avenue Foch (enter from 4 rue Rude), 75016 Paris; tel. 01 44 17 67 00; fax 01 44 17 67 50.

New Zealand embassy: 7 ter rue Léonardo-da-Vinci, 75116 Paris; tel. (01) 45 00 24 11; fax (01) 45 01 26 39.

South Africa consulate: 59 quai d'Orsay, 75443 Paris Cedex 07; tel. 01 53 59 23 23; fax (01) 47 53 99 70.

United Kingdom embassy: 35 rue du Faubourg-Saint-Honoré, 75008 Paris; tel. 01 44 51 31 00; consulate: 16, rue d'Anjou, 75008 Paris; tel. 01 44 51 31 40; fax 01 44 51 31 27.

USA embassy: 2 avenue Gabriel, 75008 Paris; tel. 01 43 12 22 22. Consulate: 2 rue St. Florentin, 75001 Paris (same tel.); fax (01) 42 66 05 33.

EMERGENCIES *(urgence)*

For 24 hr assistance anywhere in France dial:

Police (*police secours*)	17
Fire brigade (*pompiers*)	18
Ambulance (SAMU)	15

Paris has an efficient anti-poison centre: tel. (01) 40 37 04 04. You can get advice for other urgent medical problems by calling SOS Médecins at (01) 47 07 77 77 or the SAMU at (01) 45 67 50 50.

Police!	**Police!**
Fire!	**Au feu!**
Help!	**Au secours!**

Paris

ETIQUETTE

Be sure to say *Bonjour, monsieur* or *Bonjour, madame* (or *mademoi-selle* to an unmarried woman) to anyone you meet, including staff when you go into a small shop. It is usual to shake hands when introduced, and again on saying goodbye. French friends exchange kisses on alternate cheeks, and not just twice, but three, four, or more times.

Business people dress quite formally, and meetings are punctual and efficient. In contrast, you will not be expected to turn up too promptly for social functions. It is unusual to be invited to private houses: you are more likely to be entertained at a restaurant.

G

GAY and LESBIAN PARIS

The city has a large and visible gay community: the midsummer Gay Pride festival is a major event. Favourite bars, clubs, cabarets, and discos are concentrated in the Les Halles-Marais-Bastille strip.

GUIDES and TOURS *(see also GETTING AROUND on page 24)*

Multilingual guides and interpreters can be found through the Office de Tourisme de Paris (see page 122). Their monthly booklet *Paris Sélection* lists telephone contacts.

L

LANGUAGE

Even if your French isn't perfect, don't feel inhibited: it's better to make an effort. Never assume that people will speak English.

The Berlitz FRENCH PHRASE BOOK AND DICTIONARY covers almost all the situations you're likely to encounter in your travels; it's also available as part of the Berlitz FRENCH CASSETTE PACK. In addition, the Berlitz FRENCH-ENGLISH/ENGLISH-FRENCH POCKET DICTIONARY contains a glossary of 12,500 terms, plus a menu-reader supplement.

LOST PROPERTY (*objets trouvés*)

If loss or suspected theft occurs in your hotel, check first at the desk. They may suggest that you report the loss to the local police station (*commissariat*). Restaurant and hotel personnel will look after objects left behind; they turn over valuables to the police.

Lost property may turn up at the Bureau des Objets Trouvés, 36 rue des Morillons, 75015 Paris. If you have lost a passport, check first with your embassy, as the Bureau would transfer it there.

I have lost my wallet/handbag/passport.	**J'ai perdu mon portefeuille/sac/passeport.**

M

MEDIA

Radio and TV. You'll find Paris FM radio stations specializing in classical music, rock, and pop (their own, which tends not to travel outside France). The BBC World Service can be heard on medium and short-wave (650 on dial), BBC Radio 4 on long-wave, and The Voice of America on short-wave.

Besides regular French TV channels, most hotels have a range of cable services: CNN, Sky, BBC, and programmes from Germany, Japan, even Saudi Arabia, as well as French subscription channels (some carrying late-night explicit sex).

Newspapers and magazines (*journal*; *revue/magazine*). As well as the French press, a wide range of dailies, weeklies, and monthlies is available in English and other languages. You'll find them in kiosks and *maisons de la Presse*. *Pariscope* and *L'Officiel des Spectacles* are weekly guides to what's on. The free monthly *Paris Sélection* (available from tourist offices) lists concerts, festivals, and shows.

MEDICAL CARE (*see also* EMERGENCIES *on page 113*)

To put your mind at rest, make sure your health insurance policy covers any illness or accident while on holiday.

Visitors from EU countries with corresponding health insurance facilities are entitled to medical and hospital treatment under the

French social security system. Before leaving home, find out about the appropriate forms and formalities.

Paris has excellent doctors, surgeons, and medical facilities. Most bigger hotels or the consulates have a list of English-speaking doctors and dentists. Doctors who belong to the French social security system (*médecins conventionnés*) charge the minimum.

Two private hospitals serve the Anglo-American community: the American Hospital of Paris, 63, bd. Victor-Hugo, 92202 Neuilly, tel. (01) 46 41 25 25; and the Hôpital Franco-Britannique, 3 rue Barbès, 92300 Levallois-Perret, tel. (01) 46 39 22 22.

Chemist shops (*pharmacies*) are easily identified by the green cross they display. They are helpful in dealing with minor ailments and can recommend a nurse (*infirmière*) if you need injections or special care. There's always a chemist on night-duty (*service de garde*) and its name and address is displayed in the window of other pharmacies. The Pharmacie Dhery, 84 ave. des Champs-Elysées, tel. (01) 45 62 02 41, is open 24 hours a day (métro: George V).

MONEY MATTERS

Currency. The French franc (abbreviated F, Fr, or FF) is divided into 100 centimes (c or ct). Coins (*pièces*) come in 5, 10, 20, 50 centimes (marked ½F); 1, 2, 5, 10, and 20F. Banknotes (*billets*) come in 20, 50, 100, 200, and 500F. For currency restrictions, see page 110.

Banks and currency exchange offices (*banque*; *bureau de change*) (see also OPENING HOURS on page 118). Always take your passport when you go to change money or traveller's cheques. Your hotel may also offer an exchange service, though at a less favourable exchange rate. The same applies to foreign currency or traveller's cheques changed in stores, boutiques, tourist offices, or restaurants.

I want to change some pounds/dollars.	**Je voudrais changer des livres sterling/des dollars.**

Credit cards are widely accepted in hotels, restaurants, shops and petrol (gas) stations. VISA and MasterCard are the most prevalent. You may be able to use your card to withdraw cash from automatic teller machines (*DAB, distributeurs automatiques de billets*), but some machines only respond to French-issued "smart" cards. If your card is rejected by the machine, you can go to a bank exchange counter to obtain cash with it. Visa cardholders can call freephone 08 00 90 82 81 (no prefix) for assistance.

Traveller's cheques (with identification) and **Eurocheques** (with encashment card) are widely accepted.

Sales tax. A value-added tax (TVA) of nearly 21% is imposed on almost all goods and services, and is usually included in the price. In hotels and restaurants, this is on top of a service charge (also included).

Visitors from non-EU countries can have the TVA refunded on major purchases of goods for export (see page 83).

Do you accept traveller's cheques/this credit card?	**Acceptez-vous les chèques de voyage/cette carte de crédit?**

PLANNING YOUR BUDGET

The following prices in French francs should give you an idea of costs during a visit to Paris. However, they must be regarded as approximate; inflation in France, as elsewhere, pushes prices up.

Airport transfer. Bus to Orly 30F, to Charles-de-Gaulle 48F; train (second class) to Orly 25F, to Charles-de-Gaulle 30F. Taxi to Orly 140F, to Charles-de-Gaulle 220F.

Bicycle hire. 60F per day, plus 1,500–2,000F refundable deposit.

Car hire (international company). Renault Clio: 410F per day, 1,900F per week with unlimited mileage. Renault Safrane: 600F per day, 4,000F per week with unlimited mileage. Tax and insurance included.

Entertainment. *Discothèque* (admission and first drink) 80-150F; nightclub with dinner and floor show 400-800F; cinema 40-50F.

Guides. 800F for a half-day.

Hotels (double room with bath). ****Luxe 2,200F+; ****1,500-2,200F; *** 900-1,500F; ** 450-900F; * 200-450F.

Paris

Meals and drinks. Continental breakfast in hotel 40-150F; in café 30-60F. Lunch 90-200F, dinner 200-350F and upwards, fast-food meal 25-40F, coffee 8-12F, soft drink 10-20F, beer 20-40F, small carafe of wine 20-30F, bottle of wine 100F and up, cocktail 40-90F.

Métro (tickets also valid on buses). 8F; 10 tickets (*carnet*) 46F; weekly ticket (city, near suburbs, Monday to Sunday) 72F; monthly 243F. "Paris Visite" ticket 95F for three days, 150F for five days.

Sightseeing. Boats: adults 48F, children 20F. Monuments and museums: 25-50F (children less, or free). Museum Pass: (see page 74) 70F for one day, 140F for three, 200F for five days.

Taxis start at 15F (an extra 5F is charged at train stations and air terminals), plus about 3.50F per kilometre. You'll be charged 6F for every piece of baggage put in the boot (trunk). Night rates are higher.

OPENING HOURS (*heures d'ouverture*) (*see also* PUBLIC HOLIDAYS *on page 120*)

Avoid using lunch hours for "administrative" tasks; although the long Parisian lunch is becoming a distant memory, businesses and smaller shops may close for an hour or so, between 12 and 2:30pm.

Banks tend to open 9am-5pm on weekdays (many closing for lunch from 12 to 2pm) and close either on Saturdays or Mondays. All banks close on major national holidays and most close early on the day before a public holiday.

Main **post offices** are open 8am-7pm on weekdays and 8am-noon on Saturdays. Smaller post offices close for lunch from 12 to 2 or 2:30pm, and close at 5 or 6pm.

Grocers, bakeries, tobacconists, food shops are open from 7 or 8am to 7pm (or later, sometimes up to midnight), Monday-Saturday. Food shops are often open on Sunday morning. Small shops usually shut at lunch-time, 12:30-2pm.

Other shops, department stores, boutiques are open from 9, 9:30, or 10am to 6:30 or 7pm (sometimes later in summer), Tuesday to Saturday. They are closed Monday morning or all day Monday.

Museums are open 10am-5, 5:30, or 6pm (variable). Some, including the Louvre, are closed on Tuesdays: others close on Mondays. Major national monuments including the Arc de Triomphe, Panthéon, and Sainte-Chapelle are open daily, except certain public holidays. (See also Major Museums on page 67 and Paris Highlights on page 37.)

P

PHOTOGRAPHY and VIDEO

For detailed information on how to get the most out of your holiday photographs, purchase a copy of the Berlitz-Nikon GUIDE TO TRAVEL PHOTOGRAPHY (available in the UK only).

All types of blank video tape are available, but note that pre-recorded cassettes sold in France are not compatible with UK or US systems. Those specifically made as travel souvenirs will be appropriately marked.

I'd like a film for this camera.	**J'aimerais un pellicule pour cet appareil.**
a colour-slide film	**un pellicule de diapositives**
How long will it take to develop this film?	**Combien de temps faut-il pour développer ce film?**
May I take a picture?	**Puis-je prendre une photo?**

POLICE *(see also* EMERGENCIES *on page 113)*

The blue-uniformed police who keep law and order and direct traffic are as a general rule most courteous and helpful to visitors. The CRS (*Compagnies républicaines de sécurité*) are the tough guys, seen wielding batons and quelling demonstrations that have got out of hand. Outside Paris and other main cities, the *gendarmes*, in blue trousers and black jackets with white belts, are responsible for traffic and crime investigation.

If you need to call for police help, dial **17** (anywhere in France).

Where's the nearest police station?	**Où est le commissariat de police le plus proche?**

PUBLIC HOLIDAYS *(jours fériés)*

Public offices, banks, and most shops close on public holidays, though you'll find the odd corner shop open. If one of these days falls on a Tuesday or Thursday, many French people take the Monday or Friday off as well for a long weekend (this doesn't usually curtail activity in shops or businesses, however).

1 January	*Jour de l'An*	New Year's Day
1 May	*Fête du Travail*	Labour Day
8 May	*Fête de la Victoire*	Victory Day (1945)
14 July	*Fête nationale*	Bastille Day
15 August	*Assomption*	Assumption
1 November	*Toussaint*	All Saints' Day
11 November	*Armistice*	Armistice Day (1918)
25 December	*Noël*	Christmas Day
Movable dates:	*Lundi de Pâques*	Easter Monday
	Ascension	Ascension
	Lundi de Pentecôte	Whit Monday

Are you open tomorrow?	**Est-ce que vous ouvrez demain?**

R

RELIGION

These days, a live-and-let-live atmosphere towards religion prevails, with only occasional arguments about educational funding.

Immigration has brought sizeable Jewish and Muslim communities to Paris, as well as many other smaller groups. The Yellow Pages

(*Les Pages Jaunes*), found in most hotel rooms and at all hotel desks, list places of worship of every persuasion.

TIME DIFFERENCES

France keeps to Central European Time (GMT + 1 hr). In summer clocks are put one hour ahead (GMT + 2 hrs), coming into force from late March to end September. With this in mind, the following chart gives **summer** time differences.

New York	London	**Paris**	Sydney	Auckland
6am	11am	**noon**	8pm	10pm

What time is it?   **Quelle heure est-il?**

TIPPING

A little tip can go a long way in Paris. Service is *included* in restaurant bills. Increasingly, tips are given only as a token (5F) to show your appreciation for good service. But hotel staff expect to be tipped.

Hotel porter, per bag	5F
Hotel maid, per week	50F
Lavatory attendant	4F
Taxi driver	10-15%
Tour guide	10%

TOILETS/RESTROOMS (*toilettes*)

Public toilets come in the form of curved booths and are found all over Paris. They cost 2F to use and clean themselves after the user has left. Bars and cafés also have facilities — if you are not a customer, leave two or three francs in the dish provided, or at the bar.

TOURIST INFORMATION OFFICES (*office de tourisme*)

Before going to Paris you can obtain a lot of up-to-date information from the French National Tourist Office in your country. In Paris, you'll find the **Office de Tourisme de Paris** (Visitors Bureau) at 127 avenue des Champs-Elysées, 75008 Paris; tel. (01) 49 52 53 54; fax (01) 49 52 53 00. Staff will be able to help you with information and booking accommodation; the office is open 9am-8pm every day except 1 May. You can change money there, and buy phonecards and the Museum Pass. Other branches are located in major stations, the Eiffel Tower (May to September), and airport terminals.

For a selection of weekly events in English, call (01) 49 52 53 56. For information on the region surrounding Paris, contact the CRT Ile de France, 26, avenue de l'Opéra, 75015 Paris; tel. (01) 42 60 28 62.

There are French National Tourist Offices in these countries:

Australia: Kindersley House, 33 Bligh Street, Sydney, NSW 2000; tel. (2) 231 5244.

Canada: 1981 Avenue McGill College, Suite 490, Esso Tower, Montreal, Que. H3A 2W9; tel. (514) 288 4264; 1, Dundas St. West, Suite 2405, Box 8, Toronto, Ont. M5G 1Z3; tel. (416) 593 4717.

South Africa: Carlton Centre, 10th Floor, P.O. Box 1081, Johannesburg 2000; tel. (11) 331 9252.

UK: 178 Piccadilly, London W1V 0AL; tel. (0891) 244 123; fax (0171) 493 6594.

USA: 444 Madison Avenue, New York, NY 10022; tel. (212) 838 7800.; 645 North Michigan Avenue, Suite 630, Chicago, Illinois 60611; tel. (312) 337 6301; 9401 Wilshire Boulevard, Beverly Hills, CA 90212; tel. (213) 272 2661; 1 Hallidie Plaza, San Francisco, CA 94102; tel. (415) 986 4174; World Trade Center, N103, 2050 Stemmons Freeway, P.O. Box 58610, Dallas, Texas 75258; tel. (214) 742 7011.

TRANSPORT

Bus (*autobus*). Bus transport round Paris is efficient (and more pleasant than the métro) though not always fast. Stops are marked by red and yellow signs, with the bus numbers posted, and you'll find bus itineraries displayed under bus shelters. You can obtain a general bus route plan from métro station ticket offices.

Most buses run from 7am to 8:30pm, some till 12:30am. Service is reduced on Sundays and public holidays. Special buses for night-owls, the "Noctambus," run along ten main routes serving the capital, from 1:30am to 5:30am every hour, with Châtelet as the hub.

Bus journeys take one ticket. You can buy a ticket as you board, but it's cheaper to buy a book of tickets (*carnet*) from any métro station. (Bus and métro tickets are interchangeable.) Punch your ticket in the validating machine when you get on. You can also buy special one-, three-, or five-day tourist passes or the weekly ticket and *carte orange* (see Métro, below). Show these special tickets to the driver as you get on: **don't** put them in the punching machine. The fine for being caught without a ticket is 100F.

Métro. The Paris *Métropolitain* (*métro* for short) is one of the world's most efficient, fast, and convenient underground railway systems. It's also one of the least expensive, and it keeps growing to accommodate passengers' needs. Express lines (**RER**) get you into the centre of Paris from distant suburbs in approximately 15 minutes, with a few stops in between.

You get ten journeys for the price of six by investing in a *carnet* (book) of tickets, also valid for the bus network and for the RER, provided that you stay within Paris and don't go to outer suburbs. A special ticket called **Paris Visite**, valid for three or five days, allows unlimited travel on bus or métro, and reductions on entrance fees to various attractions. A **day ticket**, *Formule 1*, is valid for métro, RER, buses, suburban trains, and airport buses.

For longer stays, the best buy is a **weekly ticket** (*coupon hebdo-madaire*): note that validity runs from each Monday to Sunday. Be sure to ask for the *portefeuille* (ID wallet) to go with it — and have a passport photo ready to stick to it. For prices, see page 118.

Whatever your ticket, remember to collect it after putting it through the machine at the métro entrance gates (although most of the gates won't open until you do).

Métro stations have big, easy-to-read maps. Service starts at 5:30am and finishes at around 1am — it is not recommended to travel alone after about 10:30pm. The RATP (métro organisation) has an information office at 53 ter quai des Grands Augustins, 75271 Paris cedex. You can call them round the clock at (01) 43 46 14 14.

Paris

Train (*train*). The SNCF (French Railways Authority) runs fast, comfortable trains on an efficient network. The high-speed services (TGV — *trains à grande vitesse*) operating on selected routes are excellent, but more expensive than the average train. Seat reservation on TGVs is compulsory, and you have to pay for it.

The main stations in Paris are the Gare du Nord (for the Eurostar to London, and for Belgium and Netherlands), Gare de l'Est (eastern France and Germany), Gare Saint-Lazare (Normandy and Calais), Gare d'Austerlitz (southwestern France and Spain), Gare Montparnasse (western France), and Gare de Lyon (Provence, Switzerland, and Italy).

You validate your train ticket before boarding, by inserting it in one of the orange machines (called a *machine à composter* or *composteur*) on the way to the platform. If it is not clipped and dated, the ticket collector is entitled to fine you on the train.

Taxi (*taxi*). Convenient and quick, taxis are reasonably priced, though there'll be extras for putting luggage in the boot (trunk) and for pick-up at a station or airport. Also, taxis can refuse to carry more than three passengers. The fourth passenger, when admitted, pays a 10F supplement.

You'll find taxis cruising around, or at stands all over the city. Ask for a receipt if you need it (*un reçu*). Rates differ according to the zones covered or the time of the day (you'll be charged more between 7pm and 7am, and on Sundays). An average fare between Roissy-Charles-de-Gaulle Airport and Paris centre might be 220F by day, 280F at night. If you have any problems with a driver, you can register a complaint with the Service des Taxis, 36 rue des Morillons, 75732 Paris; tel. (01) 45 31 14 80.

TRAVELLERS WITH DISABILITIES

Paris was not planned with the disabled traveller in mind, though things are steadily improving: the Louvre, for instance, has several lifts (elevators) and can suggest special tours designed to ease getting round the museum. Airports are equipped to help; for Orly South telephone (01) 49 75 30 70 and Orly West (01) 46 75 18 18. At Charles-de-Gaulle, Air Assistance is at (01) 48 62 28 24. The métro's many stairs and few lifts make it difficult, but the RATP (métro, RER, and bus network) offers a *voyage accompagné* service from 8am to 8pm; someone will accompany you during your trip. Book 48 hours ahead on (01) 49 59 96 00. A similar service can be arranged with the SNCF (rail network), by telephoning the appropriate railway station. Sight-impaired travellers can obtain a Braille map of the métro from Association Valentin Haüy, 5 rue Duroc, Paris 75007; tel. (01) 47 34 07 90. It is worth getting a copy of Access in Paris, a guidebook for people with disabilities; contact Access Project (PHSP), 39 Bradley Gardens, London W13 8HE, England.

TRAVELLING TO PARIS

By air

Scheduled flights. Paris is served by two international airports, Roissy-Charles-de-Gaulle, and Orly. Average journey time between Paris and Johannesburg is 13 hours, London 1 hour, New York 7 hours (less than 4 hours by Concorde), Toronto 9 hours.

Charter flights and package tours. From the **UK** and **Ireland**: Most tour operators charter seats on scheduled flights at a reduced price as part of a package deal which could include a weekend or a couple of weeks' stay, a simple bed and breakfast arrangement, or a combined "wine tour" and visit to Paris. Among the inclusive holiday packages are tours for visitors with a common interest, such as cookery courses, school trips or art.

However, most visitors from the UK travel to France individually, either by booking directly with a ferry operator and taking a car across, or signing up for inclusive holidays which offer fly-drive and touring or self-catering arrangements.

From **North America**: ABC (Advance Booking Charters) provide air passage only (from New York, Chicago, Los Angeles, and San Francisco to Paris), but OTC (One Stop Inclusive Tour Charter) package deals include airport transfers, hotel, sightseeing, and meals.

Paris is the starting point for many tours of France. Wine tasting, gourmet, and cooking tours, as well as tours of the château country are included in package deals leaving from over a dozen major US and Canadian cities, usually on a seasonal basis (April to October) and for periods of one to three weeks. You can also choose from fly-drive and fly-rail schemes.

From **Australia** and **New Zealand**: Package deals for Paris are offered by certain airlines. You can also travel by independent arrangement (the usual direct economy flight with unrestricted stopovers) or go on a fly-drive arrangement.

From **South Africa**: Excursion fares and numerous package deals are available, including Paris among other European sights.

By car

Cross-channel operators offer plenty of special deals at competitive prices; a good travel agent will help you to find the suitable ferry for your destination. Dover-Calais is the shortest route and most convenient port from which to reach Paris.

Le Shuttle, the car transporter service through the Channel Tunnel, takes 35 minutes. The terminals are near Folkestone and Calais.

By bus

Regular services also operate from London to Paris via cross-channel ferries or the Channel Tunnel. Numerous lines link Paris with regional cities including Bordeaux, Lyon, or Nice.

By rail

All the main lines converge on Paris. On the ultra-rapid TGV trains which reach 300 km/h, reservation is compulsory. Auto-train services (*Trains Autos Couchettes*) are also available from major towns.

The journey between London (Waterloo) and Paris (Gare du Nord) takes only 3 hours by Eurostar train through the Channel Tunnel. For those who arrive by ferry at the French channel ports, frequent trains run to Paris.

Tickets. Visitors from abroad can buy a *France-Vacances Spécial* pass, valid for specified periods of unlimited travel on first or second class, with reductions on the Paris transport network and one or two days' free car rental (available with first class only), depending on the type of card.

Residents of Europe can buy an *Inter-Rail* or *Inter-Rail Plus* card which allows one month's unlimited second-class travel on most European rail networks. The under-26 Inter-Rail card is also available for selected zones of Europe (France, Belgium, Luxembourg, and Netherlands constitute one zone). The Freedom Pass is available for travel on 3, 5, or 10 days within any month, in one or more of the 26 participating countries of Europe.

People resident outside Europe and North Africa can buy a *Eurailpass* for unlimited rail travel in 17 European countries, including France. This pass must be obtained before leaving home. Anyone under 26 qualifies for the lower-priced *Eurail Youth Pass*.

W

WATER

Tap water is suitable for drinking (unless marked *eau non potable*).

WEIGHTS and MEASURES

The metric system — a French invention — is universal.

Length

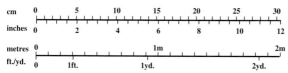

Weight

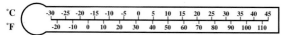

Temperature

Paris

WOMEN TRAVELLERS

As a woman alone you should not experience more problems than in most big cities. Late night public transport should be avoided.

Budget accommodation for women can be found at the Salvation Army's Palais de la Femme, 94 rue de Charonne, 75011; tel. (01) 43 71 11 27, and at several YWCAs (addresses from tourist offices) where the usual up-to-24 age rule does not apply in July and August.

YOUTH HOSTELS *(auberges de jeunesse)*

For more information, ask for the free guide to all French Youth Hostels, obtainable from the Fédération Unie des Auberges de Jeunesse (FUAJ), 27 rue Pajol, 75018 Paris; tel. (01) 44 89 87 27. For youth hostels in Paris, advance reservation is essential, year round.

Tourist information offices (see page 121) can give you a booklet *Jeunes à Paris* (Youth in Paris) with addresses and telephone numbers of hostels, student halls, etc., which provide accommodation. (Some cannot be reserved in advance.) The tourist offices may be able to arrange a reservation for you, but again, only on the same day.

UCRIF (Union des Centres de Rencontres Internationaux), 72 rue Rambuteau, Paris 75001, tel. (01) 40 26 57 64, has a number of centres in Paris. Accueil des Jeunes en France, 119 rue Saint-Martin, 75004, tel. (01) 42 77 87 80 (also in main departure hall at Gare du Nord; tel. (01) 42 85 86 19), has several hostels for young visitors.

A SELECTION
OF HOTELS
AND RESTAURANTS

Recommended Hotels

The list is divided geographically into: Right Bank — central and west (1-2, 8-9, 16-18); Right Bank — east and Ile Saint-Louis (3-4, 10-11, 19-20); Left Bank (5-7, 14-15). The numbers indicate the *arrondissement* (district), also given by the last one or two figures in the postal code, e.g. 75015 is the 15th.

The following ranges give an idea of the price for a double room, per night, with private bath unless otherwise stated. Service and tax are included, but not breakfast. Note that prices can vary widely within a hotel, and may change according to the time of year. Always confirm the price when booking.

✿	below 450F
✿✿	450-900F
✿✿✿	900-1500F
✿✿✿✿	1500-2200F
✿✿✿✿✿	over 2200F

Right Bank — central and west (1-2, 8-9, 16-18)

Baltimore ✿✿✿✿ *88-bis avenue Kléber, 75016; Tel. 01 44 34 54 54; fax 01 44 34 54 44.* 105 rooms. A modern hotel with a classic look, beautifully decorated rooms, and friendly personal service. A few minutes' walk from l'Etoile and with Boissière métro station close at hand. The prize-winning Le Bertie's restaurant offers traditional English dishes with French flair (the menu is planned by Albert Roux).

Bradford Elysées Best Western ✿✿✿ *10 rue St-Philippe-du-Roule, 75008; Tel. 01 45 63 20 20; fax 01 45 63 20 07.* 48 rooms. A friendly hotel in a peaceful street between rue du Faubourg-St-Honoré and Champs-Elysées, close to St-Philippe-du-Roule métro. A member of the Best Western reservation system.

Chopin ✿✿ *46 Passage Jouffroy (at 10 blvd. Montmartre), 75009; Tel. 01 47 70 58 10; fax 01 42 47 00 70.* 36 rooms. Situated along one of the capital's traditional covered passages (arcades) with antiques shops as its neighbours, this is a very comfortable, old-established and beautifully renovated hotel. Close to Richelieu-Drouot métro station.

Claridge Bellman ✪✪✪✪ *37 rue François-Ier, 75008; Tel. 01 47 23 54 42; fax 01 47 23 08 84.* 42 rooms. A small hotel offering the personal touch, in the stylish district lying between the Seine and the Champs-Elysées, home of many of the great names in the fashion world. The rooms are delightfully furnished with antiques. No restaurant.

Concorde-St-Lazare ✪✪✪ *108 rue St-Lazare, 75008; Tel. 01 40 08 44 44; fax 01 42 93 01 20.* 300 rooms. A classic 19th-century building listed as a national monument, and very carefully restored. Within easy reach of the Opéra, the large department stores on boulevard Haussmann, and St-Lazare station. The well-known Terminus restaurant is housed in the same building.

Hôtel de Crillon ✪✪✪✪✪ *10 place de la Concorde, 75008; Tel. 01 44 71 15 21; fax 01 44 71 15 03.* 163 rooms. The splendid classical façade of this world-famous hotel dominates the north side of place de la Concorde. Renowned primarily for its impeccable service and quality, but also for the two notable restaurants, Les Ambassadeurs and the more affordable L'Obélisque.

Dorée ✪ *66 boulevard Barbès, 75018; Tel. 01 42 23 52 36; fax 01 42 54 22 55.* 55 rooms. A pleasant, older hotel at an economical price, situated on the edge of Montmartre just below Sacré-Cœur. On a busy street but well sound-proofed. Some rooms face a quiet garden.

Ducs d'Anjou ✪✪ *1 rue Sainte-Opportune, 75001; Tel. 01 42 36 92 24; fax 01 42 36 16 63.* 38 rooms. A well-renovated older building in the middle of the bustling Les Halles district, so rooms facing the street can be slightly noisy at night.

Duminy-Vendôme ✪✪✪ *3 rue du Mont-Thabor, 75001; Tel. 01 42 60 32 80; fax 01 42 96 07 83.* 77 rooms. Just a few steps from the pleasant Tuileries gardens, this is a comfortable establishment priding itself on its attractively decorated rooms: brass beds, flowery wallpaper, and full-blown marble bathrooms.

Hôtel de l'Elysée ✪✪✪ *12 rue des Saussaies, 75008; Tel. 01 42 65 29 25; fax 01 42 65 64 28.* 32 rooms. A small and rather elegant hotel, with good views and attractive décor, in a quiet street near the presidential Elysée Palace and the upmarket shopping in rue du Faubourg-St-Honoré.

Grand Hôtel Inter-Continental ✪✪✪✪✪ *2 rue Scribe, 75009; Tel. 01 40 07 32 32; fax 01 42 66 12 51.* 514 rooms. Standing across from the Opéra-Garnier, taking up most of a triangular block, this historic hotel was opened by Empress Eugénie in 1862. It has been extensively renovated in recent years. The Café de la Paix, with its original gold and green décor restored, is a national monument. La Verrière garden restaurant occupies the lovely central courtyard.

Henri IV ✪ *25 place Dauphine, 75001; Tel. 01 43 54 44 53; no fax.* 22 rooms. A modest budget hotel, one of the very limited number of places to stay on the Ile de la Cité. Somewhat old-fashioned rooms, with shared bathrooms. Only a short walk from Notre-Dame and Saint-Michel. You will need to reserve well in advance.

Lord Byron ✪✪✪ *5 rue Chateaubriand, 75008; Tel. 01 43 59 89 98; fax 01 42 89 46 04.* 31 rooms. A pleasant small hotel, reasonably priced for its location just east of l'Etoile, with fair-sized rooms, stylish décor, and an elegant courtyard.

Magellan ✪✪✪ *17 rue J-B Dumas, 75017; Tel. 01 45 72 44 51; fax 01 40 68 90 36.* 75 rooms. Comfortable hotel in a quiet location, with an attractive garden and a sauna and exercise room. Well placed for Palais des Congrès convention centre.

Méridien Etoile ✪✪✪✪ *81 blvd. Gouvion-St-Cyr, 75017; Tel. 01 40 68 34 34; fax 01 40 68 31 31.* 1,025 rooms. Bright, modern, and efficient, and close to the Bois de Boulogne, the Air France city terminal, and the Palais des Congrès convention centre. The hotel has its own executive floor, pleasant French and Japanese restaurants, and also the Lionel Hampton jazz club with frequent visiting soloists and groups.

New Montmartre ✪✪ *7 rue Paul Albert, 75018; Tel. 01 46 06 03 03; fax 01 46 06 73 28.* 32 rooms. This is a pleasant and quite spacious budget hotel, on the eastern slopes of Montmartre just below Sacré-Cœur. Near Anvers métro station.

Regent's Garden Best Western ✪✪✪ *6 rue Pierre-Demours, 75017; Tel. 01 45 74 07 30; fax 01 40 55 01 42.* 39 rooms. A friendly small hotel in a tranquil situation just north of l'Etoile, with an attractive garden and also a fitness room. A member of the Best Western reservation system.

Terrass' Hotel ✪✪✪✪ *12 rue Joseph-de-Maistre, 75018; Tel. 01 46 06 72 85; fax 01 42 52 29 11.* 101 rooms. Long established as the leading hotel in Montmartre, set on the quiet western edge of the hill, with striking views over the capital. Indoor restaurant and piano bar, as well as La Terrasse roof-top restaurant open between May and September.

Right Bank — east (3-4, 10-11, 19-20)

Beaumarchais ✪✪ *3 rue Oberkampf, 75011; Tel. 01 43 38 16 16; fax 01 43 38 32 86.* 33 rooms. A pleasant, modernized budget hotel. Not far from the little streets and markets of the Temple quarter, and convenient for the Gare de Lyon.

Champagne Mulhouse ✪✪ *87 blvd de Strasbourg, 75010; Tel. 01 42 09 12 28; fax 01 42 09 48 12.* 31 rooms, some with balconies and some facing a quiet courtyard. A modest hotel, simply but well furnished, and recently renovated. Opposite Gare de l'Est, close by Gare du Nord, and near to a profusion of restaurants.

Crimée ✪✪ *188 rue de Crimée, 75019; Tel. 01 40 36 75 29; fax 01 40 36 29 57.* 31 rooms. Modern and comfortable. Away from the centre on the northeastern edge of the city, but good value and very convenient for La Villette (Cité des Sciences and Cité de la Musique). Close to métro station Crimée.

Des Deux-Iles ✪✪✪ *59 rue St-Louis en-l'Ile, 75004; Tel. 01 43 26 13 35; fax 01 43 29 60 25.* 17 rooms. Set in a small and attractive 17th-century mansion on the main street of the tranquil Ile Saint-Louis, this hotel is comfortable and friendly, with a cellar bar. Rooms are compact but attractively decorated. Reserve well in advance.

Grand Hôtel Jeanne d'Arc ✪✪ *3 rue Jarente, 75004; Tel. 01 48 87 62 11; fax 01 48 87 37 31.* 36 rooms. An attractive small establishment in a calm location, on the edge of the Marais near place des Vosges and the Jewish quarter. Popular with foreign visitors, and necessary to reserve in advance.

Jeu de Paume ✪✪✪✪ *54 rue St-Louis-en-l'Ile, 75004; Tel. 01 43 26 14 18; fax 01 40 46 02 76.* 32 rooms. In a delightful situation on quiet Ile Saint-Louis. The hotel has kept its ancient, 17th-century "jeu de paume" court: a game said to be the predecessor of tennis. Great for a taste of old Paris.

Libertel Terminus Nord ✪✪✪ *12 blvd. de Denain, 75010; Tel. 01 42 80 20 00; fax 01 42 80 63 89.* 245 rooms. This 1865 railway station hotel is right opposite the Gare du Nord. It was beautifully restored in 1993, and the rooms are attractively decorated and well-equipped. The balconies of some upper storey rooms look across to Sacré Cœur. The 1925 Terminus restaurant is in the same building.

Le Laumière ✪✪ *4 rue Petit, 75019; Tel. 01 42 06 10 77; fax 01 42 06 72 50.* 54 rooms. This is an excellent, value-for-money hotel, with modern, comfortable rooms, and deservedly popular. Some way from the centre, between Parc Butte-Chaumont and la Villette, close to Laumière métro station.

Lutèce ✪✪✪ *65 rue St-Louis-en-l'Ile, 75004; Tel. 01 43 26 23 52; fax 01 43 29 60 25.* 23 rooms. A small and charming hotel on the quiet, select Ile Saint-Louis, with very attractive little rooms. Those on the 6th floor are the most romantic.

Mary's ✪ *15 rue de Malte, 75011; Tel. 01 47 00 81 70; fax 01 47 00 58 06.* 38 rooms, most with private bathroom. A basic but clean and functional establishment at a budget price. Convenient for the Bastille area and its boutiques, galleries, and varied nightlife.

Paris Bastille ✪ *14 rue de la Roquette; Tel. 01 48 05 62 47; fax 01 49 23 07 58.* 30 rooms. A renovated and brightly decorated small hotel, in the heart of the Bastille district, next to art galleries, close to the Opéra-Bastille and nightlife.

Picard ✪✪ *26 rue de Picardy, 75003; Tel. 01 48 87 53 82; fax*

01 48 87 02 56. 30 rooms. A small and friendly budget hotel. Only half the rooms have private bathrooms. Located in the Temple area of little streets and old shops, looking out on the *Carreau du Temple*, site of a lively daily market.

Pyrénées-Gambetta ✪✪ *12 ave. du Père Lachaise, 75020; Tel. 01 47 97 76 57; fax 01 47 97 17 61.* 32 rooms. A quiet budget hotel on the northeastern edge of the city, close to the Père Lachaise cemetery and Gambetta métro station. A small number of rooms at a lower price do not have private bathrooms.

Saint-Laurent Gare de l'Est ✪ *5 rue Saint-Laurent, 75010; Tel. 01 42 09 59 79; fax 01 42 09 83 50.* 44 rooms. A simple, comfortable, and clean hotel, especially convenient for the stations, Gare de l'Est and Gare du Nord. There is a large and varied choice of restaurants close at hand.

Left Bank (5-7, 14-15)

Abbaye Saint-Germain ✪✪✪ *10 rue Cassette, 75006; Tel. 01 45 44 38 11; fax 01 45 48 07 86.* 46 rooms. A 17th-century abbey, situated between the Luxembourg Gardens and Saint-Germain-des-Prés, which has been beautifully adapted into a hotel. Some rooms have original wooden beams, but all modern comforts as well. The staff are helpful and attentive.

Alésia-Montparnasse ✪✪✪ *84 rue Raymond Losserand, 75014; Tel. 01 45 42 16 03; fax 01 45 42 11 60.* 45 rooms. A good base in Montparnasse, with compact but well-furnished rooms. The location is handy for the restaurants and cafés and not far from the station.

Angleterre St-Germain-des-Près ✪✪ *44 rue Jacob, 75006; Tel. 01 42 60 34 72; fax 01 42 60 16 93.* 27 rooms. A charming hotel in an historic house, with a garden. Ernest Hemingway lodged here in the 1920s.

Cayré ✪✪✪ *4 blvd. Raspail, 75007; Tel. 01 45 44 38 88; fax 01 45 44 98 13.* 119 rooms. Known for its traditional good service and unusually large rooms. Set in the attractive quarter behind the Musée d'Orsay, the hotel has long been a favourite with artists and writers.

Duc de Saint-Simon ✪✪✪ *14 rue de Saint-Simon, 75007; Tel. 01 44 39 20 20; fax 01 45 48 68 25.* 34 rooms. At the very heart of the Faubourg Saint-Germain, near the Musée d'Orsay. This is an attractively furnished early 19th-century town house that seems to come straight out of a Balzac novel. Has a lovely private garden.

Elysées-Maubourg ✪✪✪ *35 blvd. de la Tour-Maubourg, 75007; Tel. 01 45 56 10 78; fax 01 47 05 65 08.* 30 rooms. A small hotel with welcoming service and atmosphere, fine décor, and comfortable rooms. On sunny days, the tiny interior courtyard is open and makes an attractive setting for afternoon tea.

Esmeralda ✪ *4 rue St-Julien-le-Pauvre, 75005; Tel. 01 43 54 19 20; fax 01 40 51 00 68.* 16 rooms. A modest budget hotel in an old house in a fascinating part of the Left Bank, looking across at Ile de la Cité and Notre Dame. Most rooms do not have a private bathroom.

Lutétia ✪✪✪ *45 blvd. Raspail, 75006; Tel. 01 49 54 46 46; fax 01 49 54 46 00.* 273 rooms. One of the few large old, traditional recommended hotels on the Left Bank, friendly and welcoming. Its Art Deco architecture and interior design has been well preserved. The Brasserie Lutétia is popular with locals as well as visitors.

Marronniers ✪✪✪ *21 rue Jacob, 75006; Tel. 01 43 25 30 60; fax 01 40 46 83 56.* 37 rooms. A tall, narrow, and most attractive hotel with its own small garden and chestnut trees (hence the hotel's name), just one block from the place St-Germain-des-Prés with its famous cafés.

Nikko de Paris ✪✪✪ *61 quai de Grenelle, 75015; Tel. 01 40 58 20 00; fax 01 45 75 42 35.* 779 rooms. A modern and well-equipped international hotel, with a swimming pool and sauna and notable restaurants: Les Célébrités, Brasserie Pont Mirabeau, and the Japanese Benkay. View over the Pont Mirabeau and the Seine, not far from the Eiffel Tower.

Palais Bourbon ✪✪ *49 rue de Bourgogne, 75007; Tel. 01 45 51 63 32; fax 01 45 55 20 21.* 32 rooms. Near the National Assembly and Rodin Museum, a fine old building with attractive, good-sized rooms. Reasonably priced for the location, it is very popular, so reserve well in advance.

Le Pavillon ✪✪ *54 rue Saint Dominique, 75007; Tel. 01 45 51 42 87; fax 01 45 51 32 79.* 18 rooms. An attractive little place on a quiet courtyard near Les Invalides. It is a former convent, so the rooms are quite small.

Relais Medicis ✪✪✪ *23 rue Racine, 75006; Tel. 01 43 26 00 60; fax 01 40 46 83 39.* 16 rooms. A small and attractively decorated hotel, with oak-beamed rooms set around a quiet courtyard with a fountain, just off boulevard Saint-Michel and close to the Luxembourg gardens.

Saint-André-des-Arts ✪ *66 rue Saint-André-des-Arts, 75006; Tel. 01 43 26 96 16; fax 01 43 29 73 34.* 33 rooms. A friendly small establishment with a lively atmosphere and a central position in the heart of the Latin Quarter. A few rooms do not have private bathrooms.

Saint Pères ✪✪✪ *65 rue des Saints-Pères, 75006; Tel. 01 45 44 50 00; fax 01 45 44 90 83.* 39 rooms. Quiet and comfortable, with modern bedrooms, this is a hotel favoured by the publishing world, who meet over breakfast in the small courtyard. Close to place St-Germain-des-Prés and its famous café terraces.

Sèvres Vaneau ✪✪ *86 rue Vaneau, 75007; Tel. 01 45 48 73 11; fax 01 45 49 27 74.* 39 rooms. A friendly small hotel, recently restored and attractively redecorated. The area is quiet, yet not far from the boulevard Saint-Germain, its cafés and bookshops.

Tour Eiffel-Dupleix ✪✪ *11 rue Juge, 75015; Tel. 01 45 78 29 29; fax 01 45 78 60 00.* 40 rooms. A bright, newly converted hotel in a quiet street, with small but attractive rooms, some overlooking a garden courtyard. Breakfast buffet in garden room. Close to Dupleix métro station.

Turenne ✪✪ *20 avenue de Tourville, 75007; Tel. 01 47 05 99 92; fax 01 45 56 06 04.* 34 rooms. A budget hotel with attractive décor and cosy rooms, offering good value for this part of the city, next to Les Invalides.

Recommended Restaurants

In this section the term restaurant includes bistros and brasseries (see pages 93-94). The price ranges quoted are per person, for a three-course dinner with a glass or two of house wine, tax and service included. Extras will send bills much higher, but conversely, a modest lunch menu can cost much less.

✪	below 250F
✪✪	250-400F
✪✪✪	400-600F
✪✪✪✪	over 600F

Right Bank — central and west (1-2, 8-9, 16-18)

Maison D'Alsace ✪✪✪ *39 avenue des Champs-Elysées, 75008; Tel. 01 43 59 44 24.* A big, classic brasserie, on the Champs-Elysées, open 24 hours a day, every day, for Alsace specialities and excellent seafood. Offers budget menus after 11:00pm.

L'Appart ✪✪ *9 rue du Colisée, 75008; Tel. 01 53 75 16 34.* Close to the Champs-Elysées, a modern bistro that looks more like someone's apartment (hence the name). The cooking is creative but not fussy: colourful salads, pan-fried fish, and calf's liver, reasonably priced wines. Closed Sunday.

Beauvilliers ✪✪✪ *52 rue Lamarck, 75018; Tel. 01 42 54 54 42.* A restaurant in the unusual setting of an old bakery and bread shop, with a terrace for outdoor dining. The menu concentrates on classic cuisine. Closed Monday at lunch-time, Sunday and public holidays.

Le Canard d'Avril ✪ *5 rue Paul Lelong, 75002; Tel. 01 42 36 26 08.* A casual and colourful bistro featuring delicious dishes from southwestern France — especially duck (as the name implies). Closed Saturday and Sunday.

Carré des Feuillants ✪✪✪✪ *14 rue de Castiglione, 75001; Tel. 01 42 86 82 82.* Alain Dutournier is one of the most acclaimed chefs in Paris and you need to reserve days ahead. His cuisine has a distinct flavour of the southwest (Armagnac). The setting is an old convent, with futuristic décor. Closed Saturday lunch-time, Sunday and August.

Chartier ✪ *7 rue du Faubourg Montmartre, 75009; Tel. 01 47 70 86 29.* This is the place for one of the least expensive meals in town, attracting noisy, happy hordes on account of its low prices and good, traditional French cooking. With loads of character and atmosphere. Open until 9pm.

Chez Pauline ✪✪ *5 rue Villedon, 75001; Tel. 01 42 96 20 70.* An old-established bistro with lots of new ideas on offer. Specialities include fine country dishes from Burgundy, game in season, and seafood including bouillabaisse with langoustines. Closed Saturday lunch and Sunday.

Chez la Vieille ✪✪ *37 rue de l'Arbre Sec, 75001; Tel. 01 42 60 15 78.* The "old woman" in the name of this establishment is Adrienne Biasin, who presided over the kitchen for several decades. Young successors continue to produce her style of French home cooking at its best: terrines, savoury tarts, calf's liver, and beef with carrots. Open at lunch-time only. Closed Saturday, Sunday, and August.

Chiberta ✪✪✪ *3 rue Arsène-Houssaye, 75008; Tel. 01 45 63 77 90.* This elegant restaurant just beside l'Etoile has a very faithful local clientele. Closed Saturday, Sunday, all August, and holidays. Chef Philippe da Silva's style is classical haute cuisine.

Conti ✪✪✪ *72 rue Lauriston, 75116; Tel. 01 47 27 74 67.* The chef here, formerly with the celebrated Troisgros brothers, is noted for his interpretations of Italian dishes — working wonders with pasta. Closed Saturday, Sunday, and public holidays.

Copenhague ✪✪ *142 avenue des Champs-Elysées, 75008; Tel. 01 44 13 86 26.* Close to l'Etoile, this restaurant serves Danish and other Scandinavian specialities, including game and reindeer. Closed Sunday and August. The Flora Danica delicatessen and snack bar downstairs is less formal and open daily.

La Brasserie Fauchon ✪✪ *26-30 place de la Madeleine, 75008; Tel. 01 47 42 60 11.* The best-known quality food shop in Paris offers a choice of restaurants on its premises. Look round the store to sharpen your appetite beforehand. Closed Sunday.

La Fermette Marbeuf ✪✪ *5 rue Marbeuf, 75008; Tel. 01 47 20 63 53.* Worth a visit for the Art Nouveau setting in the back room, with ceramics and cast-iron columns, as well as for the food, emphasizing the finest fresh farm produce. Open daily.

Flo ✪ *7 cour des Petites Ecuries, 75010; Tel. 01 47 70 13 59.* The fame of this traditional brasserie in a little back street has spread: now it runs branches in various parts of Paris. The original serves good seafood, Alsace specialities, and brasserie standards. Budget menu after 10:30pm. Open every day until 1:30am.

Le Grand Véfour ✪✪✪✪ *17 rue de Beaujolais, 75001; Tel. 01 42 96 56 27.* Set in a gorgeously ornate late-18th-century salon in the Palais-Royal, where Napoleon once took dinner with Josephine. In contrast, Guy Martin's cuisine is modern, light, and imaginative. Closed Saturday, Sunday, and August.

Guyvonne ✪✪✪ *14 rue de Thann, 75017; Tel. 01 42 27 25 43.* Guy Cros likes to cook fish, and you can choose from six or seven kinds on the menu, depending on arrivals. Offal and country fare are also worth noting. Closed Saturday and Sunday.

Le Manoir de Paris ✪✪✪ *6 rue Pierre-Demours, 75017; Tel. 01 45 72 25 25.* A delightful Belle-Epoque setting for contemporary cuisine. Upstairs, La Niçoise serves delicious Provençal dishes in a substantially lower price range. Closed Saturday lunch-time and Sunday.

Café Marly ✪ *Palais du Louvre, 93 rue de Rivoli, 75001; Tel. 01 49 26 06 60.* You can rest from your labours in the Louvre in these Second-Empire-style rooms, facing the pyramid or the skylit Cour Louvre. Snacks, lunch, and dinner served. Open daily from 8:00am to 2:00am.

Brasserie du Café de la Paix ✪ *12 blvd. des Capucins, 75009; Tel. 01 40 07 30 20.* Traditional brasserie food, cheerfully served in the remarkable and historic setting of this 1862 café; vast, gilded, and mirrored, adjoining a covered terrace opposite the Opéra-Garnier. Open daily.

Le Perroquet Vert ✪ *7 rue Cavalotti, 75018; Tel. 01 45 22 49 16.* A casual bistro which has been a Montmartre institution for over a century, serving simple country food at an economy price. Closed Saturday lunch-time and Sunday.

Pharamond ✪✪ *24 rue Grande-Truanderie, 75001; Tel. 01 42 33 06 72.* In an authentic Belle Epoque setting, this restaurant serves a range of fine Normandy cuisine, turning the lowliest offal and giblets as well as great seafood into divine dishes. Closed Sunday, and Monday lunch-time.

Au Pied de Cochon ✪✪ *6 rue Coquillière, 75001; Tel. 01 42 36 11 75.* Bright and cheerful restaurant and terrace, in the Les Halles quarter, open 24 hours every day. Specialities are fish, big seafood platters, and pigs' trotters stuffed with truffle pâté as well as budget-priced set menus.

Right Bank — east (3-4, 10-12)

Benoît ✪✪✪ *20 rue St.-Martin, 75004; Tel. 01 42 72 25 76.* Traditional cuisine bourgeoise in a real bistro that has barely changed since its foundation in 1912. This is a popular place and you need to book days in advance. Closed Saturday, Sunday, and August.

Au Châteaubriant ✪✪ *23 rue de Chabrol, 75010; Tel. 01 48 24 58 94.* The French poet Jacques Prévert was a regular here, and the décor is enhanced by fine paintings. The cooking is Italian-influenced with seafood pastas a speciality. Closed Sunday, Monday, and August.

Chez Julien ✪ *1 rue Pont Louis-Philippe, 75004; Tel. 01 42 78 31 64.* A friendly family-run bistro in a 19th-century bakery, with home-style food. Closed Saturday lunch, Sunday, and Monday lunch.

Dos de la Baleine ✪ *40 rue des Blancs Manteaux, 75004; Tel. 01 42 73 38 98.* A little restaurant in the Marais run by two cheerful chefs offering new interpretations of country cooking at very reasonable prices. Closed Saturday lunch and Sunday.

Brasserie l'Européen ✪ *21 bis blvd. Diderot, 75012; Tel. 01 43 43 99 70.* Specializes in shellfish, especially oysters in season, but also snacks and bistro standards in the Bastille area. Open daily 11:00am to 1:00am.

Le Café Moderne ✪ *19 rue Keller, 75011; Tel. 01 47 00 53 62.* A young team in an old bistro offers heart-warming cuisine, such as black pudding and Morteau sausage, as well as lighter fare like salmon tartare. Closed Sunday.

Terminus Nord–Brasserie 1925 ✪ *23 rue de Dunkerque, 75010; Tel. 01 42 85 05 15.* In the fine 19th-century building facing the Gare du Nord, a classic brasserie, noted for its seafood and Alsace country cooking. Open daily from 11:00am until 12:30am.

Les Voyageurs ✪ *1 rue Keller, 75011; Tel. 01 48 05 86 14.* Grilled fish and shellfish at reasonable prices are the specialities of this friendly restaurant near place de la Bastille. Closed Saturday lunch-time and Sunday evening.

Left Bank (5–7, 14–15)

Le Bistrot de Paris ✪✪ *33 rue de Lille, 75007; Tel. 01 42 61 16 83.* 1900-style bistro, with a lovely billiard room on the first floor. Owner Michel Olivier (a TV chef) lives up to his excellent reputation. Closed Saturday lunch-time and Sunday. Book well ahead.

Le Bistrot d'André ✪ *232 rue Saint-Charles, 75015; Tel. 01 45 57 89 14.* This used to be the local bistro for the workers of André Citroën's car factory; it belonged to the great man himself. Entirely decorated with old documents, it's the perfect set-

ting for traditional French cooking, such as beef bourguignon.
Closed Sunday.

Les Bookinistes ✪✪ *53 quai des Grands Augustins, 75006;
Tel. 01 43 25 45 94.* A brightly-coloured modern version of a
bistro, established by celebrated chef Guy Savoy as a more
moderately priced alternative to his restaurant in the 17th
arrondissement. Imaginative starters, fish tartares, and polenta, pastas, and salads. Closed Saturday lunch and Sunday.

La Bûcherie ✪✪ *41 rue de la Bûcherie, 75005; Tel. 01 43 54
78 06.* Wonderful situation right opposite Notre-Dame cathedral. Classical cuisine: several notable fish dishes and *filet de
boeuf.* Friendly service. Open daily.

Jacques Cagna ✪✪✪✪ *14 rue des Grands-Augustins, 75006;
Tel. 01 43 26 49 39.* On the first floor of an old Parisian mansion, with sturdy beams in the ceiling and still-life paintings
adorning the walls. Noted for its marvellous fish and shellfish
dishes. Closed Saturday lunch-time and Sunday. You need to
book well ahead for dinner.

La Cagouille ✪✪ *10 place Constantin-Brancusi, 75014; Tel.
01 43 22 09 01.* Very popular restaurant, famous among fish-lovers for its simple, quality dishes and fresh ingredients.
Modern décor. Situated in the Montparnasse quarter. Open daily
except between Christmas and New Year.

Café du Commerce ✪ *51 rue du Commerce, 75015; Tel. 01
45 75 03 27.* This vast informal restaurant-cum-café is a Paris
institution, with its glass roof, pot plants, and scurrying waiters.
Open from midday to midnight, every day, for anything from a
beer to a full-scale dinner at a budget price.

Le Divellec ✪✪✪ *107 rue de l'Université, 75007; Tel. 01 45
51 91 96.* Named after its chef, a Paris personality, this first-rate
restaurant is a great favourite with politicians and media people.
Celebrated for its simple but succulent seafood and beef. Closed
Sunday.

Chez Françoise ✪✪ *Aérogare des Invalides, 75007; Tel. 01
47 05 49 03.* Chez Françoise is a favourite rendezvous for

French Parliamentarians. The restaurant specializes in seafood, game, and smoked meats. Open daily.

Lipp ✪✪ *152 blvd. Saint-Germain, 75006; Tel. 01 45 48 53 93.* Everyone who's anyone in Saint-Germain-des-Prés has a table here, and the place is filled with tourists, too. Not to be missed for a view of the neighbourhood eccentrics. Brasserie fare — Alsace country cooking, notably stews and choucroute. Open daily until 2:00am.

Paul Minchelli ✪✪✪ *54 blvd. de la Tour Maubourg, 75007; Tel. 01 47 05 89 86.* A relative newcomer to the Left Bank, this modern, cheerful restaurant has a name for some of the best seafood in Paris. The menu changes daily at lunch and dinner, depending on the catch. Reservations essential. Closed Monday.

Perraudin ✪ *157 rue Saint-Jacques, 75005; Tel. 01 46 33 15 75.* A favourite with students. Serves a range of tasty country cooking in the Latin Quarter: andouillette, beef bourguignon, and tarte Tatin. Closed Saturday and Monday at lunch-time, and Sunday.

Le Petit Zinc ✪✪ *11 rue Saint-Benoit, 75006; Tel. 01 46 33 51 66.* Once an institution in its crowded old rooms, it now glories in its "new" premises, a 1900 Art Nouveau building in the heart of Saint-Germain. Noted for magnificent seafood platters. Open every day until 2:00am.

La Truffière ✪✪ *4 rue de Blainville, 75005; Tel. 01 46 33 29 82.* A charming little restaurant in a vaulted cellar, specializing in traditional country cooking, including cassoulet and confit de canard, with reasonably priced inclusive menus. Closed Monday.

Jules Verne ✪✪✪✪ *2nd floor, Eiffel Tower, 75007; Tel. 01 45 55 61.44.* Offers a fine view of Paris and cuisine and prices to match the altitude. Exciting modern décor by Slavik. Lobster fricassé and escalope of foie gras are specialities. Open daily for lunch and dinner. Be sure to reserve well in advance.